Charles & Diana

A 10th Anniversary Celebration

Charles & Diana
A 10th Anniversary Celebration

RACHEL MARK CLIFFORD

PHOTOGRAPHS BY JOHN SHELLEY

WH SMITH

EXCLUSIVE
· BOOKS ·

ACKNOWLEDGEMENTS

Photographs on the following pages are reproduced by kind permission:
p. 5 (Lord Snowdon/Camera Press)/JS Library; pp. 8, 10 and 11 Alpha/JS Library.

This edition produced 1991 exclusively for W H Smith Ltd by
Book Connections Limited, 47 Norfolk Street, Cambridge CB1 2LE

A CIP catalogue record for this book is available from the British Library.

Designed by Tim McPhee and Elaine Tye
Design and production in association
with Book Connections Limited, Cambridge

Typeset by Cambridge Photosetting Services, Cambridge

Printed and bound in Singapore

ISBN 0 906782 53 8

FRONTISPIECE: Charles and Diana visited botanical gardens during their second tour of
Australia in 1985. Here they are enjoying its beauties among luxuriant foliage.

*R*oyal marriages have always created a furore of interest and have invariably brought instant fame to the newcomer who weds into the world's most prestigious and long-lasting royal family. The marriage of Charles, Prince of Wales and for many years the world's most eligible bachelor, was, however, the one everybody had been waiting for. When, on 24th February 1981, his engagement was at long last announced, virtually every other item of news that week faded into the background as the searchlight of interest focused on the wife-to-be whom he had taken so long in choosing.

Lady Diana Spencer, youngest daughter of the eighth Earl Spencer and his first wife, Frances, and a distant relative of Sir Winston Churchill, was nineteen years of age to Charles's thirty-two and, it was quickly agreed, admirably fitted the bill for future Queen Consort of England. She was pretty, but not too glamorous. She was unassuming and modest. She was young and fresh-faced. Unlike

*E*nter Diana – officially! Lord Snowdon, who has been responsible for numerous royal pictures, was called in for this photograph taken during Charles and Diana's engagement. Unusually, it is casual and relaxed, with Charles and Diana wearing matching shirts.

some other candidates touted over years of speculation as Charles's choice of a wife, Diana had no previous entanglements of the sort that might embarrass the Royal Family. Charles had been broken-hearted, it was said, when one girlfriend he loved dearly and may well have wished to marry turned out to have a rather talkative and vengeful former lover. With that, the relationship had to end and the prince was obliged to seek a new attachment elsewhere.

Lady Diana, however, had never gone in for the 'liberated' life style. Unusually for a well-born young woman of her class and privilege, her greatest pleasure was helping with three-year-olds at the Young England kindergarten in London and looking after a young American boy whose parents worked in the capital. It was all charmingly old-fashioned. It seemed evident that, whereas other aristocratic young ladies might expect, almost casually, to marry in the normal course of things, for Lady Diana marriage and children were a positive preference. Doubtless no one who knew Diana was surprised when, on her engagement to Prince Charles, she publicly announced that she wanted 'lots and lots of children'.

Prince Charles had long ago expressed a desire to marry 'someone British', so Diana fitted that bill, too, and most important of all, as the public soon perceived, the couple were very

Diana attends the wedding of one of her former flatmates, Caroline Pride, in 1982. With exemplary discretion, Caroline and other friends kept secret what they knew about Diana's engagement to Prince Charles. None of them breathed a word before the official announcement.

much in love. Dynastic unions, contracted for political, financial or other practical reasons, had long ago gone out of fashion. They had been effectively killed off over a century earlier by Charles's great-great-great-grandmother, Queen Victoria. Mutual affection at the least had been the vital criterion in the marriages of her nine children and their children after them. It set a standard. Today, as far as the public is concerned, nothing less than a love match will do.

All the same, Prince Charles was not entirely free to follow his heart in his choice of a wife and consort. As heir to the throne who, on becoming king, will be Head of the Church of England, he was barred under the Act of Settlement of 1701 from marrying a Catholic.

L ady Diana Spencer at her first Ascot with the Royal Family in 1981. Her red outfit is quite fussy and youthful compared to her svelte appearance in later years.

L ady Diana visited a school with Prince Charles on one of her early public appearances during their engagement. On a similar occasion at this time, an eighteen-year-old schoolboy, in a fine gesture of gallantry, held on to Diana's hand when introduced to her, raised it to his lips and kissed it.

He could do so only by renouncing his rights. That more or less ruled out his marrying a princess. Two world wars and several revolutions had decimated the royal houses of Europe and most of those which survive are Catholic. The problem was underlined by the fact that the last fully royal princess to marry into the British Royal Family was Marina of Greece, who wed the Duke of Kent, father of the present Duke, in 1934. The tabloid news-papers, which had been marrying Charles off since he was three years old, had clearly overlooked the narrowness of the prince's options.

Another obstacle was the Royal Marriage Act of 1772, originally de-signed to curb the cavortings of Hanoverian princes. Under this law, Charles could not marry without the sovereign's consent or, failing that, the agreement of both Houses of Parlia-ment. Although this approval need not apply after he became twenty-five, it was hardly likely that Charles, a loving and admiring son of Queen Elizabeth II and Prince Philip, would seek to marry without it.

Diana, wearing a frilly blue outfit, attended her first Trooping the Colour ceremony in June 1981. She is shown on the balcony at Buckingham Palace after the ceremony with the Queen Mother (right) and other mem-bers of the Royal Family. (RIGHT)

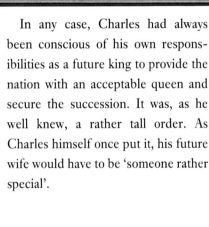

In any case, Charles had always been conscious of his own responsibilities as a future king to provide the nation with an acceptable queen and secure the succession. It was, as he well knew, a rather tall order. As Charles himself once put it, his future wife would have to be 'someone rather special'.

*I*t was ironic that in the event, Charles did not have to search far, if at all, for the wife he needed, for Lady Diana Spencer had already been around the edges of his life for many years. Born on 1st July 1961, she had been brought up at Park

The first moments of a royal marriage. Diana, now HRH The Princess of Wales, emerges on the arm of her brand-new husband as the couple leave St Paul's Cathedral on their wedding day, 29th July 1981. (LEFT)

House, on the Queen's Sandringham estate in Norfolk where she became the childhood friend of Charles's younger brothers, Prince Andrew and Prince Edward. At that stage Charles, over a decade older than this trio of young chums, was an admired senior, not remote, but rather too far on in age to join their fun.

Just how much attention Charles paid to Diana in those early days is questionable. Their first meeting is supposed to have been in 1961, when the twelve-year-old Charles was among the local gentry who paid their respects to the infant Diana. She was then only days old. Charles himself first remembered Diana much later, in 1977 when, as a 'rather splendid' sixteen-year-old, she was introduced to him by his then girlfriend and Diana's elder sister, Lady Sarah Spencer.

Sarah herself was the centre of wedding speculation the following year, when Charles turned thirty. A

remark he had once made, about thirty being a good age for him to take a wife, came home to roost, and Sarah happened to be the girlfriend of the moment. She, however, had no intention of marrying Charles. She was not in love with him, even though she thought him a 'fabulous person'. Nothing happened and speculation fizzled out.

Two years later, it started up again when Charles and Diana were seen dancing at a ball held by the Duke of Richmond, and showed an obvious interest in each other. Shortly afterwards, Diana was at Cowes on the Isle of Wight where members of the Royal Family were attending the annual yachting week. Prince Andrew was there; so were Princess Alexandra's children, and Charles, who received a ducking in the Solent when Diana sneaked up on him while swimming and overturned his windsurfer. Later that summer, when the Royal Family were at Balmoral for their annual holiday, Diana was invited to spend a weekend with them.

With other members of the Royal Family, Charles and Diana came out onto the Buckingham Palace balcony to acknowledge the greetings of the crowd that crammed the streets outside. Eighty-eight years had passed since the famous balcony saw its first royal bride, Princess May, later Queen Mary, consort of King George V.

Charles and Diana about to get into an open landau for the drive back to Buckingham Palace. The newlyweds were cheered all the way. (RIGHT)

As far as Charles's family and Diana's were concerned, none of this was unusual. The Spencers had long been close to the royals, both socially and officially. They were, in fact, precisely the sort of family – aristocratic, well-connected, respectable and with long-standing roots in Britain – from whose ranks royals were likely to choose their friends. For good measure, the Spencer ancestry included two seventeenth-century kings, the brothers Charles II and James II, most of the great noble families of England and the renowned hero John Churchill, Duke of Marlborough, who led British armies to famous victories in the early eighteenth century. The lineage was impeccable. More recently, Diana's father had been an equerry to the Queen and both her grandmothers were ladies-in-waiting and close personal friends of the Queen Mother. Diana, therefore, was no outsider. She had often been invited to join in Royal Family celebrations, such as Princess Margaret's fiftieth birthday party in

1980, and was so much part of the royal set-up that she called the Queen by her childhood name, Aunt 'Lilibet'.

Nevertheless, during that Balmoral weekend in 1980, it appears that Charles and Diana forged a new friendship of their own. They spent much time together, just walking, talking and going fishing in the beautiful grounds set among the spectacular scenery of the royals' Scottish home. Later, there were telephone calls to Diana's London flat, a bunch of red roses, several secret meetings at the homes of friends whom Charles could trust to be discreet – and a fresh upsurge of press interest.

In the next few days, Diana was pursued, much to her embarrassment, by hordes of reporters and photographers who camped outside her flat and surrounded the nursery where she worked. Buckingham Palace was soon firing off denials, which no one seemed disposed to believe, as well as protests that the press was harassing the hapless young lady. Diana's mother, Mrs Frances Shand-Kydd, had to make an impassioned appeal to the press for her daughter to be left alone or if not that, then treated with greater consideration. However, it was only the following February, when the betrothal was officially announced, that the Royal Family was able to give Diana their formal protection. She entered

While on honeymoon at Balmoral, Charles and Diana agreed to meet photographers for a special photo call at Brig a' Dee on the edge of the Balmoral estate. Asked what she thought of married life, Diana replied: 'I can recommend it!'

Clarence House, the home of the Queen Mother, where it was planned she would live until the wedding day, fixed for 29th July 1981.

Prince Charles, a romantic and thoughtful man, had proposed to Diana in an appropriate setting, a candle-lit dinner, but he took care not to hide from her the true nature of the prospects he was offering. The outside world had always seen Prince Charles as a wonderful 'catch'. He was rich – his private income from the Duchy of Cornwall alone brought in over £770,000 in 1981, and as heir to the throne he had the best promotion prospects in the land. He owned a country mansion, Highgrove House in Gloucestershire, which was worth about £1 million, including its surrounding land. He had apartments in all the royal palaces and a further, if smaller, country retreat at Wood Farm, near Sandringham. This, of course, was a very hard-nosed assessment of Prince Charles and made him look more like an investment portfolio than a prospective husband. The truth was that the material prospects were far less important than the nature of the man and his role in British life, and Charles made sure that Diana understood what might lie ahead of her if she married him.

There would be tedium, he told her, lack of privacy, frustrating restrictions and a need for security and protection which by their very nature could prove isolating. There would also be great pomp, pageantry, much adulation, constant deference and many responsibilities. This was the reality behind the tag of the world's most eligible bachelor which Charles had carried for so long and much of it, he seemed to fear, would be unwelcome to a young girl whose own life experience so far had necessarily been slender.

Already, several of his girlfriends had shrunk from the limitations that would cramp the style of a young woman with ambitions of her own. Lady Jane Wellesley, a woman with a brilliant career ahead of her in television, was one who baulked at this prospect, even though she was for

Two months before the birth of Prince William in 1982, Charles took Diana to the Scilly Isles for a short springtime holiday. The Scillies have close connections with the Duchy of Cornwall, the private estate which Charles owns as heir to the throne. When he becomes king, Prince William will inherit the duchy which was first formed in 1337 to provide the heir with a suitable income. (LEFT)

Diana, seen here leaving St Mary's Hospital, Paddington, with Charles and their day-old son Prince William, was the youngest royal mother this century when she gave birth on 21st June 1982. Ten days later, Diana celebrated her twenty-first birthday. (RIGHT)

Diana's mother, Mrs Shand-Kydd and her father Earl Spencer arrive at the hospital to see their new grandson, Prince William, in 1982. Earl Spencer and the Hon. Frances Roche married in 1954 but were divorced after fifteen years in 1969. Diana has two elder sisters, Jane and Sarah, and a younger brother, Charles. All of them, like Diana, are now married with children of their own. Sadly, though, there was a brother Diana never knew. He was called John and he died in infancy in 1960, a year before Diana was born. (BELOW AND RIGHT)

many years the bookies' favourite to marry Prince Charles. Another was the firebrand Anna Wallace, who was far too independent and tempestuous to knuckle down to the role Charles required of his princess. Anna stalked out of the Queen Mother's eightieth birthday party in 1980 because Charles was apparently not paying enough attention to her. The woman Charles sought had to have much greater propriety than this and also had to be, potentially at least, well tuned to the public service aspect of royal life. Far from having a personal star to pursue, she had to be willing to make being Princess of Wales her career.

Knowing all this, Charles thought it both wise and fair to ask Diana to think things over – 'in case it would be too awful' – on an already planned twelve-day visit to Australia with her mother. The precaution was unnecessary: Diana never had any doubts. In fact, she returned early from Australia, after only ten days.

'Of course I accepted,' she told journalists when interviewed about her engagement. 'I think he's terrific! Who wouldn't?'

To judge by the ecstatic reaction which greeted the betrothal, no one else had any doubts about it, either. The Royal Family was said to be delighted. Charles was beaming and could now put behind him the lonely evenings which he had sometimes spent solitarily in his apartments. Who but the most churlish anti-monarchist could have been anything but happy that a well-loved, much-admired prince now had the prospect of marriage and a family of his own?

The British people have always been generous towards newcomers marrying into their Royal Family and Lady Diana Spencer was by no means the first recipient of an excited welcome. She was the first prospective Princess of Wales for over seventy years, since the previous holder of the title became Queen Mary on the accession of her husband as King George V in 1910. Diana would also be the first bride of a Prince of Wales since Princess Alexandra of Denmark arrived in England to marry the future King Edward VII in 1863. However, statistics apart, Diana prompted appreciation in her own right. People liked what they saw and liked it on sight. Here was an attractive, unpretentious girl, unsophisticated and rather young for her nineteen

Royal grandmother for the third time. The Queen emerges from the hospital after seeing the new-born William, her second grandson and third grandchild. (ABOVE)

Proud father. Charles arrives at St Mary's Hospital, Paddington, to see his new-born son and heir, William. 'Give us another!' chanted the crowd when they saw him. 'Give us a chance!' the Prince shouted back in good-humoured reply. (RIGHT)

The traditional way of announcing births in the Royal Family is a notice signed by the doctors who attended. This is the framed announcement of the safe delivery of Prince Harry on 15th September 1984. (INSET)

BUCKINGHAM PALACE

Her Royal Highness The Princess of Wales was
safely delivered of a son at 4.20 PM today.

Her Royal Highness and her child are both well.

Signed

8th September 1984

years with an endearing habit of blushing visibly when embarrassed. Despite her aristocratic lineage, she projected a girl-next-door image that made her appear much like the daughter of an ordinary family, and the way in which crowds greeted her when Charles appeared with her in public indicated instant and enthusiastic approval of his choice.

At this early stage, Diana did, of course, have much to learn about life as a public figure. Fortunately, everyone was more than willing to sympathise with her as, rather gauchely, she took her first steps into the searchlight of curiosity which has long illuminated the lives and doings of royals. Naturally, she made mistakes. One was the very low-cut evening gown she wore to attend a theatre on her first public engagement. When she realised the gaffe, she cried with embarrassment on the shoulder of Princess Grace of Monaco. Later on, while watching Charles play polo, Diana found the batteries of press cameras beamed on her were just too much, and she fled in a flurry of tears. The lesson there was that where royals go, cameras follow. Unfortunately, even ten years on, at nearly thirty, Diana has not yet become used to the cameras in the sense that she still feels uncomfortable under the scrutiny of dozens of lenses. Even so, she has at least learned to be photographed – and she is today the world's most photographed woman – without prompting a remark she

received in her early days in the public eye. Seeing how Diana shut her mouth tight, probably from nerves, one press cameraman called to her: 'Come on, love, we're not going to take your teeth out!'

Luckily, Diana had plenty to think about at this time, in the run-up to the wedding, the most exhilarating period of this young girl's life. Royal engagements are never very long and by the time the publicity over Charles and

During their Australasian tour of 1983, Charles and Diana showed off Prince William to New Zealanders during a crawl-about on the lawns of Government House, Auckland. Diana had to get down to basics with her son to stop him crawling off on his own during the photo session.

Diana's engagement had subsided, preparations for the wedding were already well in hand. Early in March 1981, it was announced that the venue was to be St Paul's Cathedral, rather than Westminster Abbey which had seen centuries of royal weddings. There was some disappointment over this, but it appears that Charles and Diana thought the Abbey too small for the 2,650 guests they intended to invite. The bonus was that, since St

Paul's was further from Buckingham Palace than the Abbey, this allowed more pavement space for the enthusiastic crowds to occupy. Besides this, Charles wanted his wedding to be accompanied by fine music and St Paul's had the better acoustics. In the event, some of the most accomplished musicians in Britain – members of the Royal Opera, Covent Garden, the Royal Philharmonic and English Chamber orchestras, of which Charles was patron, as well as the New Zealand soprano Kiri te Kanawa – took part in the service.

The wedding plans included other breaks with tradition, too. The promise to obey was going to be omitted from Diana's vows – the Prince and his fiancée were, it was said, a modern-minded couple – and an unknown duo of fashion designers, David and Elizabeth Emmanuel, supplanted the long-established royal *couturier* Norman Hartnell as the makers of the wedding dress. The Emmanuels, whose style was feminine and romantic, had already made quiet progress into the wardrobes of the Duchess of Kent and her sister-in-law

Prince William on photo call at Kensington Palace in 1983. At one point, he decided the session was over and made a dash for the door, only to be rapidly retrieved by Prince Charles. (LEFT)

During the photo call at Kensington Palace in 1983, Prince William became curious about one of the big TV video cameras. (RIGHT)

Prince William on his swing in the garden of Kensington Palace in 1983. Charles stands behind him, ready to set the swing in motion. Despite his busy life and many preoccupations, the Prince of Wales always tries to find time to play with his children. (INSET)

Diana, who was expecting Prince Harry at the time, opened the new Harris Birthright Research Unit for Foetal Medicine at King's College Hospital in July 1984. (LEFT)

Prince William looks warily at the battery of photographers invited to Kensington Palace for a photo call in 1983. As his parents well know from their own experience, camera lenses are a constant presence in royal lives. The photo call, which is strictly limited in place and time, has proved a good way to introduce young royals to the inevitable. (RIGHT)

Royal mothers together. The Princess of Wales and Princess Michael of Kent keep an eye on their children at the Trooping the Colour ceremony in June 1984. Diana was expecting Prince Harry, who was born three months later. (BELOW)

Happy parents for the second time around. Charles and Diana leave St Mary's Hospital, Paddington, in September 1984 after the birth of Prince Harry. People were amazed at Diana's smart appearance. In her elegant red coat, she looked more like a woman who had been to a fashion show rather than one who had given birth less than twenty-four hours previously.

Princess Michael, as well as several show-business personalities. They first came to Diana's attention when she saw one of their blouses, a shell-pink chiffon creation with a high frilled neck. The Emmanuels had already put a lock on the door of their salon in Mayfair, London, as security for their designs and they were to need it as, in deepest secrecy, they set to work on Lady Diana's wedding gown.

Meanwhile life and work for the Royal Family Firm, as King George VI once called it, went on more or less as usual. Even for Prince Charles, impending marriage could not interrupt royal duty. At the end of March, he had to leave for a long-planned tour of Australasia, Venezuela and the United States. Diana, of course, had not been included in the arrangements and she had, as yet, no official status in the royal scheme of things. So Charles went on his own, leaving Diana with tears in her eyes as she watched his plane take off. Charles, who himself appeared upset at the parting, was away for five weeks and the couple were not reunited until 3rd May, at Craigowen, an old lodge on the Balmoral estate.

Charles returned from abroad to find the run-up to his wedding had advanced rapidly in those five weeks. Gifts had poured in – from a heart-shaped potato from a young school-child, to a magnificent matching set of sapphire cuff links, and sapphire brooch, bracelet and necklace from the Royal Family of Saudi Arabia. In all, Charles and Diana received over 4,000 wedding presents, of which only a quarter was put on show for the 200,000 people who came to view

Flowers for the new royal mother. St Mary's Hospital was swamped with flowers and messages of congratulation when Diana gave birth to Prince Harry in the famous Lindo Wing. William and Harry were both born in the same room in the Wing. (ABOVE)

Big brother. Prince William arrives with his father to see his younger brother Harry for the first time. The two boys have turned out to be rather different in temperament – William boisterous and mischievous, Harry quieter and less prone to pranks, unless William eggs him on, of course. (RIGHT)

Charles and Diana, with Princess Anne (left) and their children, seen on the balcony at Buckingham Palace watching the Sovereign's Birthday Parade in 1985. Harry, in Prince Charles's arms, is not paying much attention to the proceedings, but in the front row, William and two friends find plenty of interest. (OVERLEAF)

William, like most children, needed some encouragement on his first day at a west London kindergarten in 1985. Charles and Diana look on as Jane Mynors, head of the school, talks to the young prince. The Prince and Princess of Wales have always thought it important that their sons mix with children of their own age, and both William and Harry have been taken to public playgrounds and swimming pools so that they can be with ordinary children for a time. The big difference, though, is that the two princes must have a detective with them for security. (ABOVE)

Harry on his first day at school in 1987 seems very keen to start lessons. William, an old campaigner when it comes to classes, takes his duty as elder brother seriously and places a restraining arm on Harry's shoulder. Prince Charles used to look after his younger sister Anne in much the same way when they were children. (LEFT)

Charles and Diana were delighted when their two boys joined them on the royal yacht *Britannia* at the end of their Italian tour in 1985. Diana dislikes leaving her sons, but duty calls often and she has to be away from them from time to time. Sometimes, she stays behind while Charles is touring so that they will have at least one parent at home. (ABOVE)

A family moment in the front garden of Harry's first school. Charles, Diana and William look on as Harry engages the headmistress in conversation. (RIGHT)

William and Harry climbed all over this fire engine on the Sandringham estate in 1988, and Prince Harry is about to make sure the warning bell works. (OVERLEAF)

Everyone wants to join in. Watched by Charles, Diana and the Queen, Peter and Zara Phillips – Princess Anne's children – prepare to climb aboard the fire engine. (ABOVE)

Diana loves all children, not just her own, and like Charles, she has a special sympathy for handicapped youngsters. Here she is in February 1982 talking to a young spastic boy when she visited the Charles Chaplin Playground for Handicapped Children, named after the famous Hollywood comedian. (LEFT)

Mother and son. Prince Harry sits on mother's lap during a royal holiday in Spain in 1988. Diana, whose own parents were divorced when she was nine, has been determined to forge a secure family life for her children and is more involved than most royal mothers in their day-to-day upbringing, including their games and their holidays. (RIGHT)

Prince William is pictured at Windsor in March 1989 with his mother and the Duchess of York (right). The three were returning to Windsor Castle with the rest of the Royal Family after an Easter service at St George's Chapel.

them at St James's Palace. Security advisers – a group who were to become all too familiar in the couple's future life together – had warned against a more lavish display.

Royal weddings in Britain have been splendid shows of pageantry, excitement and rejoicing ever since they went public, as it were, with the marriage of the future King George v and Queen Mary in 1893. Before that,

royal marriages had been private, family affairs, usually celebrated at St George's Chapel, Windsor. In total contrast, Charles and Diana's wedding turned out to be a world-wide bonanza. Countries of the British Commonwealth, joined by several foreign countries, issued a matching series of postage stamps, an 'omnibus' to mark the occasion. For Britain's set of wedding stamps, showing a portrait of the couple framed in silver, Charles had to stand on a box to raise him above Diana, since there was only an inch or so difference in their height. This made room on the stamps, above Diana's head, for the Queen's profile which appears on all British stamp issues. There were Charles and Diana coins, Charles and Diana drinking mugs, Charles and Diana bookmarks and numerous other special wedding products. A big firework display was arranged for the wedding eve and television prepared for record viewing figures. Statistics later revealed that eight out of ten viewers in Britain had watched the wedding broadcast, either live or in the form of recordings shown in the evening. World-wide, some seven hundred million people watched Charles and Diana get married, one hundred million more than viewed the first landing on the moon twelve years earlier.

Tourists and sightseers poured into London. The wedding took place at the peak of the tourist season, and in 1981, the capital's hotels were bursting with visitors. One lucky American family rented an apartment opposite St Paul's, which gave them a grandstand view of the proceedings from the balcony. A television crew was there to record their emotion and excitement as, far below, the bride emerged on Charles's arm, no longer simply Lady

Diana but the Princess of Wales. Diana was now Her Royal Highness, a prefix long reserved for the wives of princes in line of succession to the throne.

Charles looked as splendid as his bride, in his naval No. 1 ceremonial dress uniform, one of forty uniforms which were part of his regular wardrobe, complete with royal-blue sash, orders and ceremonial sword. Predictably, the Emmanuel wedding dress – in taffeta with full scallop-edged skirt, big puff sleeves, deep-frilled neckline and enormously long train – was a sensation and set the standard for other brides who followed Diana to the altar in the second half of 1981. As soon as Diana emerged from the famous Glass Coach at the foot of the stairs leading up to St Paul's Cathedral, artists and designers were busy sketching the dress from television pictures and the first replica was

Remembrance Day (ABOVE). Charles (front), Prince Philip (centre) and the heavily bearded Prince Michael of Kent (right), all in service uniforms, stand behind the Queen at the Cenotaph in London's Whitehall in November 1984. At this sad and solemn annual ceremony, the royals lay wreaths at the Cenotaph in remembrance of Britain's war dead. Other members of the Royal Family watch, clad in black, from a balcony above. The picture below shows (left to right) King Olav of Norway, a grandson of King Edward VII and therefore a relative of the Royal Family, whose country fought alongside Britain in the Second World War; the Princess of Wales; Princess Anne; Princess Alice of Gloucester; and the Queen Mother. The red flowers are Remembrance Day poppies.

Diana and Charles and their two sons (centre) join the rest of the Royal Family on the balcony at Buckingham Palace to see the fly-past after the Trooping the Colour ceremony in 1990.

in a West End shop window that same afternoon.

Despite, or maybe because of, the millions of eyes that were watching and the scores of microphones ready to pick up every whisper, both Charles and Diana seemed very nervous. Both made mistakes during the service. Diana got Charles's names in the wrong order – 'She's marrying my father!' quipped Prince Andrew, the best man – and Charles endowed her

with all her worldly goods instead of his own. Nobody minded. It simply added charm and a human touch to the solemnity of a great public occasion.

Afterwards, as Charles and Diana rode back to Buckingham Palace in an open carriage, not an inch of pavement was to be seen as crowds crammed the streets, cheering, waving and shouting out greetings. The whole route was a sea of Union Jacks, streamers and festive hats, a vista of gaiety and joy that

Diana rides with the Queen Mother to the Trooping the Colour ceremony at London's Horse Guards Parade in 1985. The ceremony is part of the celebrations for the Queen's official birthday in June. It is so arranged that soldiers from all regiments have a share in honouring the anniversary each year. (ABOVE)

At the Queen's official birthday in 1982, the Queen (left), Prince Philip (centre), Prince Charles (right) and the Duke of Kent (far right) all wear ceremonial uniform. As Princess of Wales, Diana, standing on Charles's right, was attending the occasion for the first time. When this picture was taken of the royals on the balcony at Buckingham Palace, the birth of Prince William was less than a fortnight away. (BELOW)

belied the grey and overcast weather. Later, there were more ecstatic crowds waiting to see the newly-weds emerge onto the balcony at the Palace where, by tradition, the Royal Family shares its celebrations with the public. The now-regulation kiss, made before thousands of delighted eyes, received roars of approval. The public was still massed on the pavements as evening approached, to see Charles and Diana, who was wearing a shining pink going-away outfit, set off for Waterloo Station to spend the first few days of their honeymoon at Broadlands, the Hampshire home of the Mountbatten family. This was followed by a Mediterranean cruise in the royal yacht *Britannia* and a further ten weeks with the rest of the Royal Family at Balmoral.

In September Diana had her first experience of the Braemar Games, a regular engagement for the Royal Family during their summer break in Scotland. Charles, more sombrely, had to break off the honeymoon early in October to go to Egypt as the Queen's representative at the funeral of the murdered president, Anwar Sadat. The occasion was all the

The Queen Mother's ninetieth birthday on 4th August 1990 was one of the great royal celebrations of the year. The royals turned out in force to help the Queen Mother celebrate and here they are outside her home, Clarence House. Prince Philip (left) stands next to Princess Anne, the Princess Royal, with Diana and Charles next and Princess Margaret standing far right. The Queen Mother, still spry and active despite her great age, is out in front with the Queen. (PREVIOUS SPREAD)

The Queen Mother amuses Charles and Diana at the Braemar Games in 1984. The royals attend the games in early September most years during their annual summer break at Balmoral. The games have special relish for the Queen Mother, who is a Scot by birth. (ABOVE)

Charles, Diana and other members of the Royal Family emerge from St George's Chapel, Windsor, after the Christmas Day service. Since this picture was taken in 1984, the demands of security have stopped the royals appearing on the church steps all together as they are here, in case they present too good a target for possible attack. Instead, they leave in ones and twos by side doors, well out of sight. (RIGHT)

Diana made her first appearance at the Braemar Games in September 1981 during the last part of her honeymoon with Prince Charles at Balmoral. As a compliment to the Scots, she wore a pretty two-piece tartan outfit with matching beret. (LEFT)

Diana attended the Braemar Games in 1983 in a smart green velvet suit while Charles wore his kilt, as he usually does when in Scotland. Charles and Diana have an important connection with Scotland in common – they are both descended from the last king of a separate Scotland, King James I, who became King of England as well in 1603. (BELOW)

more distressing because Charles and Diana had entertained Sadat on board *Britannia* during their cruise, and with his wife Jehan, the president had seen the royal couple off when they flew home to Britain in mid-August. Charles was back, however, within three days.

*B*y the end of October the new Princess of Wales had officially ended her honeymoon and was ready to start work as a public figure and the latest recruit into the Royal Family Firm. During her engagement and at the time of the wedding, Diana had already experienced a taste of the royal variety of fame, but the basic characteristics of that fame, despite all Charles's warn-

ings, were yet to be fully revealed to her. It was, as she soon discovered, a curious mixture of adulation, intrusion, demanding curiosity, being constantly stared at, being on show to hundreds or thousands of people at one time in a way no other kind of celebrity has to endure. Even film stars have more privacy, as well as fewer obligations to their public. Add to that the scores of cameras recording the scene, with long lenses probing every facial angle and revealing virtually every pore. Facial expressions would be minutely observed, signs of tiredness or boredom instantly noticed. If the day was hot, and Diana was to roast in tropical climates while on tour, there could be no sign of discomfort, or if cold, no hint of shivers. Clothes would be scrutinised for fashion pointers. Hair and make-up must

*C*harles chats with guests at a Buckingham Palace garden party in 1987. Although it may not look like it, this picture was taken from the roof of the palace where photographers covering the event are normally sited.

be pristine. Royals cannot afford to look untidy or dishevelled. Deportment must be correct. Royals must not slouch. Above all, there was the high expectation of crowds and onlookers, who had often waited long and impatiently for a glimpse of a royal visitor and must not be disappointed. There was also that finely balanced trick of exchanging a few words when someone was presented, then knowing how to finish the encounter in seconds to move on to the next person. All in all, in their public life, royals could be

Children presenting flowers are a regular part of life, and a very pleasant one, for royal ladies. Here, the Queen, the Queen Mother and the Princess of Wales receive bouquets from two Scots lads. (ABOVE)

Charles and Diana about to leave by car after attending Christmas morning service at Windsor in 1982. (RIGHT)

Charles and Diana enjoy a break at Windsor at Easter 1989. In this picture, they are joined by Zara Phillips, Princess Anne's daughter, and their son William, as they return from church. (LEFT)

Charles and Diana view the blooms at the Chelsea Flower Show in 1984.

Charles and Diana view the blooms at the Chelsea Flower Show in 1984.

forgiven for feeling like specimens under a microscope.

Prince Charles, of course, was thoroughly accustomed to all this and had long ago taken for granted that being royal meant that his life must be regimented. This was not a concept that came easily to Diana, whose life until marriage had been relatively free and uninhibited. To an extent her parents had spoiled her, possibly because their divorce in 1969 made Diana the child of a broken home. Fortunately, they did so without turning her into a brat. As Lady Diana Spencer, she had done much as she liked with few restraints, though happily what she liked to do – have fun with her friends, look after children, go shopping – was nothing outrageous.

Now, as the wife of the heir to the throne and a future Queen Consort, Diana had graduated into an entirely different league, full of duties, obligations and restrictions, with a diary that detailed virtually hour by hour where she had to be and what she had to do.

Diana was fortunate to have an old campaigner like Charles on hand to guide her through her first, admittedly awkward days in the public eye. He moved easily under the barrage of interest that had long been focused on him and had already perfected the art of remaining friendly and relaxed, while at the same time retaining his royal dignity. Diana could hardly have had a better mentor and even before their marriage, Charles was showing her some of the tricks of the royal trade. It was Charles, for instance, who told Diana how to get lost in traffic in order to shake off pursuing reporters. It was Charles who, on their engage-

ment day, advised his fiancée to say the first thing that came into her head when quizzed by the press so that there would not be an awkward silence while she searched for words.

Even so, Diana had to endure pressures early on in her married life from which even Prince Charles could not protect her. The chief pressure came from the fact that the new Princess of Wales was hot news, so hot that she found it very hard to handle. Newspapers and magazines the world over clamoured for pictures of and stories about her. Where no hard facts could be gleaned – and there were few at this stage – stories were invented. It soon

William gets a cuddle from mother as Diana and her elder son relax at a polo match in July 1989. Diana likes watching polo, which is an exciting game, but she worries about its dangers. (RIGHT)

became a truism that a publication with Diana's picture on the cover sold out in hours, and to a large extent this is still true. Consequently, photographers lurked everywhere – outside Highgrove House, down at the shop in the nearby village of Tetbury where Diana bought sweets. They lay in wait for her by her car, watched the garden for her to appear and even managed to penetrate the rooms at Highgrove with powerful telescopic lenses. Later, when Diana was on holiday in the Caribbean, photographers even hid in the bushes to snap her in her bikini. Virtually the only place Diana was safe from the attentions of the press was Buckingham Palace, where she and Charles were living until their own London home, a double apartment in Kensington Palace, was ready for them.

The situation got so much out of hand that the Queen, through her press secretary, Michael Adeane, summoned national newspaper and TV and radio news programme editors and representatives of the big news agencies to Buckingham Palace. There, Michael Adeane impressed upon his audience the fact that Diana was becoming despondent and unsettled at the thought that she could hardly open her own front door with-

Charles escorts Diana between chukkas at a polo match. This picture was taken six days before the birth of Prince William in June 1982. (LEFT)

Charles relaxes between chukkas while he chats with another polo enthusiast, his great-uncle Earl Mountbatten. Mountbatten (right) was a great influence in his life and Charles, who adored him, was heartbroken when the Earl was murdered by the IRA in 1979. (RIGHT)

Discussing tactics at a polo match in 1982. Charles (front left) plans strategy with his polo manager, Major Ronald Ferguson, the father of Sarah who is now Duchess of York. (LEFT)

All kitted out and ready to go, Charles checks his horse's bridle before a game. The protective helmet which all polo players wear is very necessary. Players have suffered some nasty injuries, as Charles himself discovered in 1990.

Charles in action at polo, about to make a strike. The game was introduced to the royals by Earl Mountbatten after he saw it played in India, where he went as Viceroy in 1946. Both Mountbatten and his nephew Prince Philip were enthusiastic polo players in their time. (LEFT)

Charles paid a painful penalty for his love of polo when he had a bad fall, resulting in a broken arm, in the summer of 1990. Here he is, a short while later, out of action and 'grounded' with his arm in a sling at the Sandringham Flower Show. (ABOVE)

out being confronted by the press. In other words, the whole thing had become an obsession and it must stop.

To their credit, the media heeded this appeal to gallantry and human kindness. With a few exceptions, they agreed to relax the pressure and confine their activities to Diana's public engagements. The sacrifice, if it was sacrifice, was not all that great. There were ample photo opportunities on those engagements and better ones than the sneak pictures the media had previously wrung from an unwilling subject. It was, in the first place, inevitable that Diana would afford photographers far more smiles and pleasantness as they tracked her on walkabout, shaking hands among the crowds which came to see her and chatting happily to those lucky enough to be immediately behind the barriers that lined the walkabout route.

Also, as was equally inevitable, Diana began to confine her 'Sloane Ranger' fondness for casual clothes – jeans, bright sweaters, baseball caps, boots – to the off-duty part of her life and in public stepped easily into a royal role that had been more or less vacant: as a fashion trendsetter. This tradition went back a very long way, six or seven centuries, to the time when kings and their consorts were the natural leaders of fashion. Diana's own ancestor, King Charles II, had revolutionised fashion in 1660 after his return from twelve years of exile in Europe, and Charles's great-great-grandfather, King Edward VII, had been known as a 'snappy dresser' despite his well-

Diana hands over the trophy after a polo match, while a beaming Prince Charles looks on.

The Princess of Wales and the Duchess of York walking to-gether at Ascot in 1987. The two are friends of long standing and Diana was delighted when Sarah Ferguson be-came her sister-in-law in 1986. Diana, in fact, indulged in a bit of match-making on behalf of her friend. Sarah, the livelier of the two, often encour-ages Diana into joint pranks. The two of them once wolf-whistled at Prin-cess Michael of Kent and on another occasion, they poked a friend in the behind with an umbrella. (PREVIOUS SPREAD LEFT)

Charles escorts the Queen Mother at Ascot in 1987. Charles has always been close to his grandmother, whom he admires enormously, though she has not been able to impart to him her compulsive brand of love for horses and racing. Charles is a com-petent rider and was heart-broken when his favourite mount collapsed and died after a race in 1981, but the real stars of royal horsemanship are the Queen and Princess Anne. (PREVIOUS SPREAD RIGHT)

The younger royals take a skiing holiday most years, and make it a family affair. Charles, Andrew and their wives are shown at Klosters in Switzerland in 1987. This was the first visit they made as a royal quartet after Sarah Ferguson became a member of the Royal Family on her marriage to Prince Andrew the previous year. (ABOVE)

Cosily clad against the cold, Diana prepares to start off down the *piste* during her winter skiing holiday in Liechtenstein in 1985. The royals try to make their holiday carefree by arranging a photo call on the first day so that once the pictures are taken, the press will leave them alone.

Since 1986 Charles, Diana and their sons have spent regular holidays with Charles's distant cousins King Juan Carlos (front row, first on right) and Queen Sophia (front row, second from left) of Spain on board the king's yacht. Unfortunately, Juan Carlos and his wife were unable to attend the royal wedding in 1981 because Charles and Diana started their honeymoon cruise at Gibraltar, over which Spain and Britain have long been in dispute. (PREVIOUS SPREAD)

deserved nickname of 'Tum-Tum'. By the time Diana became Princess of Wales, royal leadership in fashion had been in abeyance for some time, and apart from the Queen Mother's famous pastels and certain outfits worn by Princess Margaret, the royal wardrobe attracted fairly minor attention.

The scene changed dramatically, and completely, after Diana first stepped out in public. She was the fashion trade's dream: taller than average and, after some dieting to lose the last of her teenage puppy fat, marvellously slender and stylish, with beautiful blonde hair and a fine complexion. Diana did not, of course, turn into a leader of fashion overnight. In her first appearances as princess, some of her skirts were too long, some outfits were unduly fussy, some evening gowns a bit girlish and certain colours, like deep plum or dark green, were too ageing for a twenty-year-old. But Diana's sense of style matured quickly and as her twenties progressed, she carried off fashion with increasing aplomb. Fashion-followers, however, did not wait for Diana to mature. They began copying her from day one. When Prince Charles went to Australia in March 1981, during their engagement, he was confronted with a bevy of Diana look-alikes, all with blonde hair cut short and sporting his fiancée's

heavy swirling fringe. Since she was so tall, Diana wore low heels, no more than an inch or so high. As a result, shoe-shop windows in Britain and elsewhere were soon full of low-heeled footwear. Likewise pearl chokers, culottes, puff-sleeved blouses, high necks, frills, tiny feathered hats – none of them extraordinary or innovative in themselves – came back into fashion simply because Diana wore them.

The Prince of Wales goes windsurfing during Yachting Week at Cowes on the Isle of Wight. Windsurfing takes strength, balance and nerve, just the sort of sporting challenge Charles likes best. Labelled 'Action Man' when younger, the prince has gone in for a wide variety of sports, all of them adventurous.

The first people to meet Diana as Princess of Wales on tour were, appropriately enough, the people of Wales. In her first big public engagement, Prince Charles took his new young wife to his principality for a three-day visit and found himself well and truly upstaged. The Welsh were all agog to see Diana and during public appearances those not on her side of the street were visibly disappointed when they got Charles instead. Charles took it all in good humour and revealed that he was working on a scheme to divide his wife in two so that everyone could meet her.

As for Diana, she entered into the spirit of the tour with almost too much enthusiasm. She shook so many hands that her own quickly became red and sore, and she learned the hard way that pressing the flesh, as hand-shaking is termed, has to be done more economically. In addition, Diana stopped so often to talk to people in the crowd that the timetable was in danger of being overturned.

There is little doubt that the Welsh were delighted with Diana, that she gave every appearance of enjoying herself and that Prince Charles was mightily proud of her. It was soon noticed that he would gaze admiringly at Diana whenever he got the chance, and that he looked more relaxed and happy than ever before. There was,

even so, a less pleasant aspect to the tour of Wales. Welsh nationalists displayed banners reading 'Go Home Diana' and 'Go Home English Prince', and security was as tight as a barnacle on a ship's keel. It was just as well, for firebombs were discovered at Pontypridd and Cardiff. However cheery and outgoing the main action of the tour, in Charles and Diana's immedi-

Diana buys moccasins at the Burghley Horse Trials in 1989. The anonymous pre-marriage days when she could pop down the King's Road, Chelsea, and buy herself a pair of jeans or a T-shirt are gone, of course, but Diana still enjoys shopping whenever she can.

ate surroundings security was on the alert in every conceivable position. Manhole covers and letter boxes were sealed along the royal route. Policemen stood guard at road junctions. The royal car was flanked front and back by police vehicles, and whenever the royal pair walked, marksmen lurked on rooftops and police with dogs prowled at ground level. It was, as far as human ingenuity could make it, blanket security cover and however unobtrusive to those who paid more attention to the joyous aspects of the royal visit, it was nothing unusual on a tour. Neither Charles nor Diana gave any sign of nerves or worry over it, but they were nevertheless well aware that royals were targets not only for greetings and popular admiration but also for those of more sinister intent.

Back in London, Diana was soon introduced to that standard royal task, tree planting. She planted her first tree in London's Hyde Park in November 1981 and early that same month attended the State Opening of Parliament, riding in the Glass Coach with her sister-in-law Princess Anne. That day, 4th November, there was a special radiance about Diana which had already been noticed and diagnosed by two nurses at a hospital she had previously visited. Seeing the rosy glow in Diana's cheeks, the nurses guessed she was expecting a baby. Their guess was confirmed the day after the State Opening, when the royal pregnancy was announced officially.

Diana was unfortunate in being one of those women who have a hard time in early pregnancy, over and above what can normally be expected. There was great sympathy for her when she appeared pale and washed-out on a tour in York where, in spite of everything, she insisted on climbing aboard one of the trains at the railway museum. November also saw Diana switch on the Christmas lights in London's Regent Street, her first solo appear-

On holiday in Spain with their parents, Prince William makes faces at the camera while Prince Harry, the quieter of the two, sits solemnly by. In their pranks together, William is always the ringleader, but he is very protective towards his younger brother. (LEFT)

Resplendent in cerise gown and insignia, Prince Charles attends a service at Westminster Abbey in May 1990 for members of the Order of the Bath, one of several ancient royal orders to which he belongs. (RIGHT)

ance in public. There were other engagements, in Northampton, in London and on a further visit to Wales, and it was not until April 1982, two months before her child was due, that Diana retired temporarily from public life.

Prince Charles greeted the prospect of fatherhood with great excitement and pride. He soon proved himself modern-minded and according to Diana read every book about pregnancy and child-rearing he could lay his hands on. He became something of an expert, it appears, and was well able to recognise the onset of labour, at five in the morning on 21st June 1982. Prince William Arthur Philip Louis was born sixteen hours later, at 9.05 p.m. weighing in at a little over 7.5 lb. Charles was present throughout the birth and next day took mother and son back to their new London home, apartments 8 and 9 at Kensington Palace.

*P*rince William, second in line to the throne after his father, was christened in the Music Room at Buckingham Palace on 4th August, the eighty-second birthday of his great-grandmother, the Queen Mother. Unlike his father, who had slept through the whole thing, William had quite a lot to say for himself at his christening and had to be quietened by his mother, who stuck her little finger in his mouth for him to suck.

Charles takes the salute at a march-past of guards in 1981. Ceremonies like this, complete with famous bearskins and red coats, are an important part of the royal pageantry for which Britain is renowned throughout the world.

Normally at this stage, after the initial publicity about birth and christening, royal infants tend to disappear from public view. They re-emerge months later, standing, however unsteadily, on their own two feet and completely transformed from the blanket-wrapped bundle first pictured on leaving hospital. Prince William, however, proved to be the exception when, breaking all precedent, his parents took him to Australasia in

March 1983 at the age of nine months. William was a large bouncy baby, very active, with fingers everywhere and Diana was utterly devoted to him. So much so that when the Australasia tour was planned, she insisted that William go too, instead of being left behind in England as was normal. This was how, against all established practice, Prince William became the youngest royal ever to go on an official tour abroad.

Royal officials and advisers were

Prince Charles, a qualified pilot, has often flown his own helicopter or aircraft to public engagements. (ABOVE)

Charles deep in discussion at a game fair where he tried his hand at clay pigeon shooting. Diana prefers her husband to shoot at inanimate targets like these because she dislikes blood sports. (RIGHT)

When ships of the Task Force returned home from the war in the Falkland Islands in 1982, Charles went on deck to welcome the troops home. Prince Andrew was a combatant in the fighting and Charles confessed he was a little wistful that, unlike his younger brother, he never saw action during his own time in the Royal Navy. (ABOVE)

Someone in the crowd who came to see Charles open the Glamorgan Nature Centre in 1982 gave him a daffodil for his lapel. The daffodil is the national flower of Wales. (OVERLEAF, LEFT)

The Princess of Wales, seen here with an armful of flowers, visited Glebe House in Kidlington near Oxford in February 1989. (OVERLEAF, RIGHT)

Tricks with colourways. Diana wore this deep-blue jacket with black collar, trimmings and skirt when she went to Wembley in 1986 to present prizes at the Young Engineers for Britain Competition. The black and blue were reversed on the jacket worn by Diana at Toynbee Hall in January 1990 when, as patron of Help the Aged, she visited the Senior Leisure Care Centre in East London.

Diana takes the salute at the Combined Cavalry 'Old Comrades' annual parade and memorial service in Hyde Park, London, in May 1989. (RIGHT)

Charles and Diana arrive in glittering style to attend the President of India's banquet in London's St James's Court Hotel in April 1990.

Diana arrived clad in this brilliant tartan outfit to visit the College for Disabled Children at Froyle in 1989. In a television interview with Prince Charles, Diana remarked that having two healthy boys of her own made it all the more important for her to work on behalf of less lucky children. (LEFT)

Diana's tour of Wales in 1981 was her first major outing as a member of the Royal Family. She is seen arriving at Aberdyfi station, to find a large and enthusiastic welcoming party waiting for her. The twenty-year-old Diana is rather girlishly dressed in plaid coat with black velvet trimmings and matching beret, in total contrast to the glamorous figure of more recent years. (ABOVE)

People often seize up with nerves on meeting royalty, but Prince Charles is an old hand at putting them at their ease. Here Charles is enjoying a good laugh with Rod Stewart and Rick Parfitt of Status Quo during a public engagement in 1985. (OVERLEAF)

Thousands turned out to see Diana on her first tour of Wales in 1981. Here she is greeting someone in the crowd on what was, unfortunately, a very windy and rainy day. Diana lost her battle with her umbrella and ended up looking bedraggled. So did her neat little feathered hat. It has never happened again. Now, Diana always looks beautifully turned out, whatever the weather.

Charles met the people of his principality as a married man for the first time when he took his new wife to Wales in 1981 on a three-day getting-to-know-you tour. He had to take a back seat for once. It was Diana whom the Welsh people were anxious to see, but it was evident to everyone that he was enormously proud of her. (LEFT)

Diana did too much handshaking on her first big public tour, to Wales in 1981. After three days, her own hand was red and sore, and she often fell far behind Prince Charles on walkabout because of the delay. (BELOW)

Diana is often given flowers when out on public engagements. Some are formal bouquets, but many others are small bunches of blooms from people in the crowd, like this little Welsh boy, who want to show their pleasure at seeing the princess. Often, the flower-giving goes too far – Diana's lady-in-waiting and personal detective have to help out and become loaded down with bouquets. (ABOVE)

The Princess of Wales and Cardinal Basil Hume at Westminster Cathedral in May 1989 for the Festival of Flowers and Music, held in aid of the Cardinal's refuge centre for young people at risk in London. Here Cardinal and Princess talk shop: work to aid and protect the young is something both are familiar with.

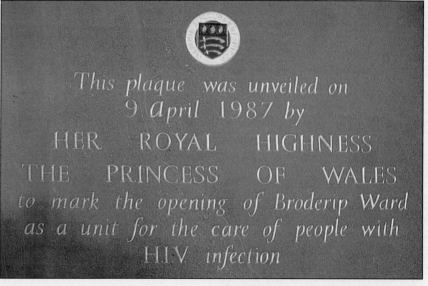

This plaque was unveiled on
9 April 1987 by
HER ROYAL HIGHNESS
THE PRINCESS OF WALES
to mark the opening of Broderip Ward
as a unit for the care of people with
HIV infection

Diana braves another rainy day in January 1989 to visit Dr Barnardo's, of which she is president. This was a post she took over from Princess Margaret.

Diana leaves her mark with this plaque erected in 1987 to commemorate her opening of the HIV ward in a London hospital. She created a sensation by sitting with patients and shaking their hands at a time when there was a big scare about the dangers of HIV infection, which can lead to AIDS. The picture shows her talking to the medical staff. (FAR LEFT AND LEFT)

Children have long been close to Diana's heart. She started that part of her career early, looking after her brother, Charles, who is three years younger than herself. In January 1989 she toured the College for Disabled Children at Froyle, accompanied by the Lord Mayor and several dozen enthusiastic children. (LEFT)

Handshaking is regular exercise for famous people such as the Princess of Wales. The hand being offered here, at Aylesbury in Buckinghamshire when the Princess visited in May 1989, was one of thousands shaken by Diana in the course of the year. (ABOVE)

One of Diana's less formal public engagements took place in the Edmonton district of London in July 1990, when she came to open the new police station.

said to be aghast and the Queen none too happy. Outside the Royal Family, there was no lack of criticism for the innovation. The main planks of concern were that a child as young as William could be unsettled at this break in his routine and that the visit, lasting four weeks, was taking place in the full blaze of the gruelling Australasian summer.

In the event, William was not whisked round the country on show to the public view, as critics may have envisaged. He was photographed at the start of the tour, arriving at the airport at

Alice Springs in the centre of Australia with his parents and his nanny, Barbara Barnes. He appeared, sitting between Charles and Diana, on a car drive where, to the delight of the crowds, he waved and grinned. Later, William crawled about during a photo call in the grounds of Government House in Auckland, New Zealand. For the rest, together with Barbara Barnes, and a small team of security guards, William stayed at Woomargama, deep in the farmlands of New South Wales, Australia, where his parents returned to see him at weekends. At Easter, they were able to stay a few days more. The anxiety of Charles and Diana to see their son regularly was reflected in the fact that they and their entourage flew some 40,000 miles back and forth

Diana's devotion to pop music is well known, but her musical interests also have their serious side. Here she is in February 1989 at the Barbican in London for a performance of Verdi's *Requiem* given by the London Symphony Chorus of which she is patron. (ABOVE)

Diana informally dressed for an engagement at the Savoy Hotel, London, in May 1989, where she attended a Floral Luncheon in aid of the Forces' Help Society and Lord Roberts Workshops. (RIGHT)

between Woomargama and various towns, cities and other points on the royal tour. It was less hectic when the tour moved on to New Zealand. At Auckland, the capital, Charles and Diana had the whole top floor of

Government House to themselves and over a fortnight they spent only three nights away from William.

The amount of extra organisation needed to accommodate one infant within the complexities and myriad small details any royal tour involves had, all the same, been very great. The main reason the Queen had set aside her own misgivings and allowed William to accompany his parents was that she took pity on Diana's distress at the prospect of leaving him behind. The tour did wonders for the royal reputation in Australia where talk arises from time to time of replacing the Queen and her representative, the Governor-General, with a republic, but just how much William contributed to that effect could not be assessed.

All the same, Charles and Diana did not repeat the experiment on their visit to Canada in June 1983, even though this meant being apart from William on his first birthday. When quizzed about his absence, the couple contended that their son was really too young to realise the significance of the anniversary. However, it was likely that the first birthday of their first-born had great significance for them, for Charles and

Off to the theatre for Charles and Diana when they attended a rock gala in aid of the Prince's Trust at the Dominion in Tottenham Court Road, London, in 1983. Pop concerts were an innovation in 1982 for the royals, but they have proved a tremendous success and have taken place regularly ever since. (LEFT)

If Diana adores children, they also adore her. This little boy got the hug of a lifetime when he threw his arms around Diana's neck while she was visiting the Chinese Community Centre in Liverpool. (RIGHT)

Eye-catching in shocking pink the Princess of Wales, patron, makes her way to Covent Garden, London, where on a September morning in 1990 she attended the opening of the First International Covent Garden Festival and an exhibition of stage make-up at the Theatre Museum, Russell Street. (LEFT)

Diana arrives by helicopter for her visit to the new Sony factory at Bridgend, South Wales, which she opened in April 1982. This was one of her last engagements before she retired from public life to await the birth of Prince William. (RIGHT)

Diana proved to be remarkably attentive parents. They employed nannies and nursery helpers, of course, but neither William nor his brother Prince Harry, born in 1984, was nursery-reared. Nor, as was the normal practice among royal and aristocratic families, did either grow up in relative isolation from their parents, to be viewed, well scrubbed and more or less well behaved, for an hour or so at tea time. As a mother, Diana, who breast-fed both her sons, saw them in all their moods – fretful while teething, wakeful at night and later mischievous and, in William's case particularly, boisterous as young boys eager to explore the world about them. William, a right royal little terror, as even his mother admitted, often led the more docile Harry into mischief and was once discovered egging Harry on to stuff his toys down the royal toilets. Diana, even her patience stretched, has been known to slap the royal bottom in public when William's antics went too far.

Diana also saw to it that she was there at the first milestone in her sons' lives, the start of school-days. Later, she often drove the boys to school and collected them. In September 1990,

when William went as a new boy, or 'squit', to his first boarding school near Wokingham in Berkshire, both his parents were there to see him settle in, even though Charles had left hospital only two days previously after an operation on his arm, broken in a polo accident.

Diana shopped personally for her sons' clothes, and broke completely with the royal tradition of dressing boys as girls for the first two years of their lives. It was rompers, trousers and T-shirts and formal suits as soon as William and Harry were out of baby clothes.

Both Diana and Charles quickly became adept at amusing their boys

Diana has rarely gone in for floppy hats, but here she is wearing one at St Albans Cathedral in September 1989. There, she unveiled a new window in the north transept and afterwards attended a service of thanksgiving. (OVERLEAF, LEFT)

Diana chats with an onlooker while on a visit to Newham in September 1990 when she opened the Lord Gage Centre there. (OVERLEAF, RIGHT)

An off-duty moment for Diana during the Australian tour of 1983. Diana and a former flatmate talk over old times while Diana's lady-in-waiting, Anne Beckwith-Smith (front right), looks on.

Diana steps out in a dazzling gown with tight black top and frothing red skirt at the America's Cup Ball at Grosvenor House Hotel in London's Park Lane. The America's Cup is a yacht racing trophy which US teams have won in most years that the race has been run. Charles has a particular interest in the sport as Commodore of the Royal Thames Yacht Club. (LEFT)

and when, as became inevitable, they had to be away from them on tour, William and Harry could always be sure of a telephone call before bedtime and, where possible, flying visits from mother, father or both. Charles, in fact, has driven hundreds of miles between engagements just to spend a few hours with his children. He also began to turn down public engagements at home where they would clash with the boys' bedtime. When off duty, Charles has taken them on pony rides, chased round with them on bicycles and zoomed down slides with them at an adventure playground. Quite un-

publicised, Diana has taken the boys out on treats – to the cinema, swimming at public pools, or to tea at small cafés and restaurants.

Taking William along on the Australasian tour in 1983 was, in its way, a public pronouncement that Charles and Diana meant to be active, involved parents and give the royal duty to set an example of family life a new facet of personal investment. William, however, was not the only one to experience a milestone during the royal tour of 1983. Diana had already been abroad as Princess of Wales when she went to Monaco for the funeral of

Princess Grace in September 1982. Diana had insisted on going, as a token of her admiration for the former film star who had befriended her at the time of her engagement in 1981. This, however, was more in the nature of a private visit and a brief one. Australasia saw Diana's first full-scale tour overseas. It was also Charles's first as a married man. The ground covered was already familiar to the prince. He had, after all, spent part of his school-days in Australia, and like other members of the Royal Family he was a highly experienced globetrotter. In 1983 Australians, New Zealanders, Canadians and most others who encountered him noticed that Charles had changed, and for the better. The agent of change was, of course, Diana.

Though only thirty-two at the time of his marriage, Prince Charles had already acquired a slightly middle-aged air. A thoughtful, reflective man with a deep interest in philosophy, archaeology and social issues, he had never been greatly drawn to the high-flying life style of many of his royal contemporaries. Efforts to turn him into a fashion trendsetter like his great-uncle, the previous Prince of Wales and later King Edward VIII and Duke of Windsor, failed to spark any enthusiasm in Charles. He would rather go off on a solitary painting holiday in his old smock and artist's hat than step

Diana surrounded by children, just the way she likes it. This picture was taken in Australia in 1983 when she visited the Alice Springs School of the Air where children in this remote town, like others similarly placed, receive lessons by radio.

out in style and be seen in fashionable venues. In any case, unlike his predecessor, Charles was happiest with old-fashioned values. For example, he had no time for rampant feminism, he preferred classical music to the latest hits, and his private life before marriage centred around a group of long-standing friends and much time spent with other members of the Royal Family. In his teens and twenties, Charles turned himself into a great sportsman – parachutist, windsurfer, skier, horseman – and appeared to enjoy the 'Action Man' image this gave

him. Even so, his chief activities in this area were the ones traditional for royalty – shooting, steeplechasing and in particular his beloved polo. Charles may have seemed a bit of a stick-in-the-mud to some and certainly he had never been one to set high society on fire, but the popular perception of him was quite different and much more complimentary. Apart from being caught drinking a liqueur at the age of fifteen, Charles had never seriously ruffled the calm surface of royal life, and if he was old-fashioned, the public thought this was well and good. To

them, he appeared nice, traditional, dutiful, charming and a comfortable prospect as future king. Earl Mountbatten, the great-uncle Charles adored, once remarked that it was a 'bloody miracle' that the heir to the throne had turned out to be the decent sort he was, quite unlike some of the high-jinks princes of the recent past.

Diana's life, too, had led her along some of the well-trodden paths of her aristocratic origins. The separation and, later, acrimonious divorce of her parents was a nasty, unsettling episode in her childhood and quite possibly brought home to her the importance of a good, solid marriage, the sort she meant to have for herself. Even so, the characteristics of her upbringing were largely traditional – a not very academic education, finishing school, weekends away in the country, well-heeled social life, gracious if not luxurious living and plenty of youthful fun. There were few serious obligations in a life like that, certainly nothing to compare with the duties that would later devolve on Diana as Princess of Wales, and there was a

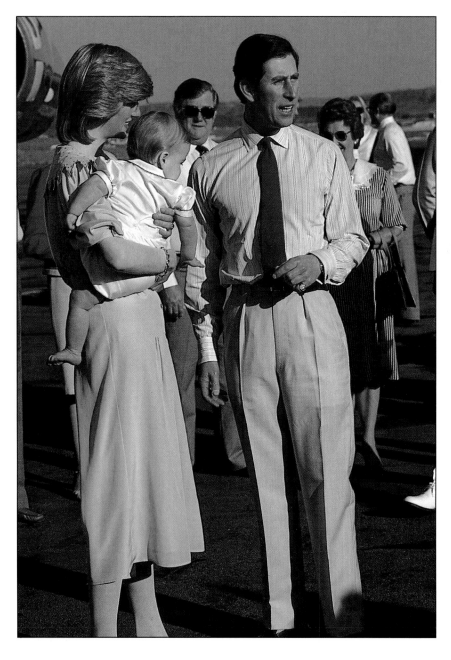

Charles, Diana and nine-month-old Prince William arrive at Alice Springs at the start of their first Australian tour in 1983. Diana could not bear the thought of leaving the infant prince behind in Britain and the Queen allowed him to be included on the tour. No royal as young as William had ever been on tour before, or since, and this first experiment was not to be repeated.

Charles, Diana and Anne Beckwith-Smith climbing the famous Ayers Rock which, next to the Sydney Opera House, is the most famous tourist venue in Australia. The largest monolith in the world, Ayers Rock rises up to 335 metres of terracotta sandstone. (RIGHT)

Charles and Diana teamed up with Australian Prime Minister Bob Hawke and his wife for this picture taken during their Australian tour in 1983.

great deal of freedom for her to follow her own tastes and interests. She was drawn to pop music, adored dancing at which she excelled, loved ballet – she wanted to be a ballet dancer until she grew too tall. She also became part of the aristocratic set known as the 'Sloane Rangers' – cotton-printed skirts, quilted jackets, neckerchief and all.

When she married a man nearly thirteen years older than herself, cast

Prince Charles, Australian flag in hand, talks to children while on walkabout in Canberra. Note the policeman standing nearby. However relaxed and friendly everyone seems, security goes everywhere with the royals. (LEFT)

by his role in life and by his own inclinations into a rather more staid mould than her own, it was inevitable that a bright young spark like Diana should seek to polish up her husband's image. Charles evidently allowed himself to be polished, because his suits began to look smarter, his socks and ties more colourful, his hair better set and his whole appearance became much neater and brighter.

The change was more than just outward show, however. It also became evident that now he was a husband and father, Charles felt able to be rather more of his own man. He was less nervous than before, lost the tic in his cheek and his gauche, tense way of standing, and stopped fiddling with his signet ring when talking to people. According to a member of his staff, marriage to Diana made Charles 'a much more warm and open person'. He was also a lot less reticent than

before about demonstrating his own inclinations.

As a young man, before he was married, Charles had cultivated an image in keeping with that of his strong-minded down-to-earth father, Prince Philip. He was by no means the first son to follow such a course, but Philip's bluff approach to life, partly the fruit of his days in the Royal Navy, made no allowance for Charles's gentle and romantic traits. Of the Queen and Prince Philip's first two children, Princess Anne, in fact, is much more like father and Prince Charles more like mother.

Once Charles and Diana married and became a distinct 'item' in their own right, Charles apparently acquired the confidence to pursue openly his interests in the more metaphysical aspects

This kangaroo seemed quite un-aware of who was looking at him when Charles and Diana, sitting in the third seat from the left, rode by in viewing carriages during the Queens-land train tour of Sunshine Plantation. The kangaroo, or 'roo for short, is the symbol of Australia and a full-grown male can stand over six feet tall.

There's no doubt about this Australian's feelings for royalty: she loves them. She was there, clad in the Australian flag with Union Jack umbrella, to greet Charles and Diana in 1983. Their tour, like others before and since, have put paid to talk of a republic, a theme that occasionally arises in Australia.

of life: organic farming, homoeopathy, holistic medicine, vegetarianism, spiritualism. At Highgrove House and on his Duchy of Cornwall estates he grew organic vegetables and laid down a wild-flower meadow of which he became extremely proud. Charles also went back to nature by shaking off his royal persona and living for brief periods as a Hebrides crofter or a Cornish dairy farmer. More publicly, Charles embarked on a series of attacks on modern architecture, taking as his cue the ugliness and destruction of aesthetic pleasure which, he con-tended, too much modern building

Thousands of Australian schoolchildren crammed the stadium at
Handy Oval Bunbury to see Charles
and Diana drive round the arena.

Diana turns and waves as she and Charles board a Royal Australian Air Force BAC 1-11 at Tennant Creek in 1983. They were on their way to Woomargama to spend precious time with their son William. (LEFT)

On her second tour of Australia with Prince Charles in 1985, Diana presented a more sophisticated image to the Australians. Her youthful charm, however, shone through – after all, she was still only in her mid-twenties. (RIGHT)

This Australian girl is chauffeuring the Princess of Wales during Charles and Diana's second tour of the country in 1985. There was no chance of her breaking the speed limit, though. The motorised cart in which Diana was travelling went at only a few miles an hour. (BELOW)

typified. Architects, Charles believed, should design 'something which is visually beautiful as well as socially useful'. Charles felt so strongly on the issue that he publicly lashed a proposed new building in London's Mansion House Square as 'a glass stump more suited to downtown Chicago than to the City of London' and in 1984 termed the new extension to the National Gallery 'a monstrous carbuncle'.

Charles's comments provoked a furore of professional protests, and the accusation that he was a reactionary yearning nostalgically for ancient architectural elegance. Others were concerned that the prince had overstepped the barriers which by tradition prevented royals from indulging in controversies, still less creating them as Charles had done. Nevertheless, Charles's outburst produced sackfuls of mail from the public in support of his contention that the best type of building, community architecture, took into account the ideas and desires of the people who had to inhabit it.

In this, Charles was showing himself to be a prince who cared about the physical environment, just as his back-to-nature interests showed concern for the natural environment. To an extent he had been led this way by Prince Philip who had campaigned to preserve the environment in the 1960s and by the Queen and the Queen

Diana wore the spectacular silver dress designed for her by former Barnardo boy Bruce Oldfield when she was the belle of a ball held in Australia during the tour of 1985. (LEFT)

Diana dances the night away with Charles at a ball which they attended during their second visit to Australia. (RIGHT)

Mother who had long preferred homoeopathic remedies to more orthodox drug-based medicine. The Queen Mother, who had shared this proclivity with her late husband, King George VI, had so much faith in homoeopathy that she gave these remedies to her horses, her 'darling boys', as she called them. Even so, none of this protected Charles from some sharp criticism in the press, and even from charges that he was eccentric, a bit of a crank and had been turned soft by marriage to Diana.

Diana, for her part, had her own environmental concerns. She had long disliked the idea of killing animals for

sport, despite the fact that shooting game was a royal and aristocratic tradition of long standing and fox-hunting was practically part of the mores of the nobility, to which she belonged. A pet-lover since she was a small child, Diana particularly disliked the habit of 'blooding' small children and she was distressed at the idea that her sons were expected to undergo this initiation into the hunting fraternity.

However, even more worrying were the number of dangerous sports in which Charles indulged. Diana was by no means the only one to be concerned. Fears were regularly voiced, in the press, about the way the heir to the throne seemed to be risking death or serious injury in the name of sport. By comparison, Diana's own sporting

Charles wears an Australian bush hat in Sydney during the third royal tour down under in 1988.

interests – swimming and tennis – were quite uncontroversial, though in 1988 the regular skiing holiday she took with Charles and other royals

tragically underlined the perils. That year, Charles and Diana's close friend, Major Hugh Lindsay, was killed in an avalanche at Klosters, Switzerland, and another friend, Patti Palmer-Tomkinson, was badly injured. Diana and Sarah, Duchess of York, were safe in their chalet at the time, having taken the afternoon off after Sarah, who was three months pregnant, took some bad falls on the *piste*. Charles, however, was with Major Lindsay at the time of the tragedy and, it was later pointed out, could just as easily have died, too. The shock was so great that Charles wept inconsolably when he realised what had happened.

Major Lindsay's untimely death did not, however, bring a halt to the royal skiing holidays but Diana did, apparently, campaign against another of her husband's dangerous activities: cross-country steeplechasing. This is a form of riding with all the characteristics of fox-hunting, but no fox and no pack of hounds to chase it. Diana made some progress with the steeplechasing after Charles fell several times from his horse, and also with the shooting, in which she hotly refused to join on a fraught occasion early on in her married life. She made no progress, though, with Charles's beloved polo, to which several of his friends had already fallen victim with some seriously broken bones. Eventually, as was inevitable, the risks claimed Charles, when he fell from his horse during a match in the summer of 1990 and broke his arm in two places. The injury proved to be very serious and an operation, involving a bone transplant taken from Charles's hip, became necessary in September 1990 to ensure that one of the fractures had the chance to heal properly. Charles left hospital after five days, looking wan, using a stick and declaring that he 'felt awful'.

There was no mention, though, of giving up polo, even though the 1990 season was obviously over as far as Charles was concerned and numerous public engagements, including a tour of Brazil, had to be cancelled. For

Charles, polo is no fad but a sport to which, like his father and great-uncle Earl Mountbatten, he is enthusiastically devoted. If anything, the dangers involved may make the whole thing more exhilarating. Six years before his accident, in fact, Charles celebrated the birth of his second son, Harry, with a polo match at Windsor where afterwards the champagne flowed on two counts: Harry's safe arrival, and the fact that his father had scored a hat trick.

As with William in 1982, Charles had stayed with Diana for the birth, at St Mary's Hospital, Paddington, and again took her home to Kensington Palace within twenty-four hours. He

Diana is not exactly out in all weathers during the course of her working life, but she sometimes comes close, as this picture taken in Australia in 1988 shows. Her hairstyle secret is a good cut and lots and lots of hair lacquer.

departed for Windsor only when he was sure Diana was being well looked after by two of the St Mary's nurses.

The new baby broke the sequence of boy first, girl second which had been started by the Queen and Prince Philip in 1948 when Charles himself was born. There was also some approval that Charles and Diana had provided the traditional heir, William, and a 'spare', Harry, and both parents were

Royals like the security that guards them to be as unobtrusive as possible, but they cannot have that wish granted all the time. Police motor cyclists, like this one who helped look after the safety of Charles and Diana in Australia, ride in front of the royal car every time it takes to the road.

Diana, her blonde hair styled up in a french pleat, dances with her husband at a ball while on tour in Australia. Diana loves dancing and is good enough to partner John Travolta, the disco film star, with whom she once danced at the White House in Washington. (BELOW)

naturally delighted with their brace of boys. Having two children made them even more distinctly a family unit.

By the time Harry was born, Diana was a sophisticated twenty-three and the smartly dressed, elegantly coiffured young woman who emerged outside the hospital with her second son in her arms was very different and much more stylish than the still girlish, round-faced twenty-year-old who had walked out to show her first to the eagerly waiting crowds. Media interest in Diana had never abated although the obsessive pursuit of 1981 and 1982 had largely lapsed. It was, however, difficult for the media to tone down their attentions when they were confronted with such an attractive prospect for news stories and pictures.

In her mid- and late twenties, a time when a woman can have the polish of maturity while still retaining the shine of youth, Diana was a striking figure, always beautifully dressed and able to carry off with ease almost any colour or

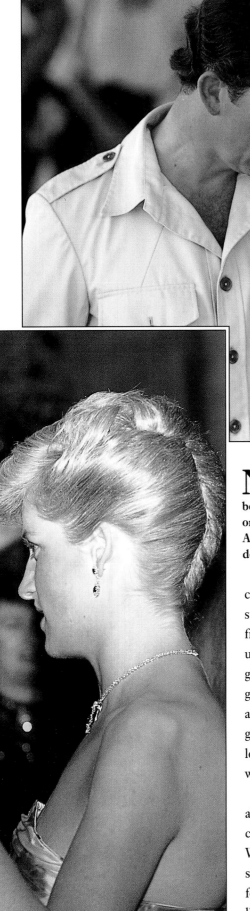

Natural history is one of Charles's keenest interests. Here he is being shown some crocodile eggs on one of the last royal engagements in Australia in 1988 before he and Diana departed for Thailand.

combination of colours. Diana enjoys superb health which gives an enviable freshness to her face and, despite an unfortunate nose, she is very photogenic. With the years, Diana had also grown in confidence and expertise, and when out together on public engagements, Charles no longer had to look behind and check that his wife was coping all right on walkabout.

He certainly had no need to worry about her on that score. She delighted crowds with small confidences about William and Harry, their doings and sayings, warming the heart of every fond mother who, like her, needed little prompting to do the same. Diana

also developed a nice line in royal small talk for encounters with the public which, of necessity, had to be brief, but must also show personal interest.

'What nice shiny medals!' she remarked, seeing an old soldier, his decorations proudly displayed on his chest. 'Did you polish them for him?' Diana asked his wife.

'My Dad says you should give me a kiss!' a young boy boldly contended on another occasion.

'Well then,' Diana replied. 'You'd better have one!'

This was not conversation of great depth – it was neither meant nor needed to be – but it achieved its purpose, to put people at their ease, raise a smile and warm hearts. It was

Diana has a private word with Charles as they watch an open-air display in Australia. (OVERLEAF)

well up to the standard set by the Queen Mother, that prime exponent of the art. The children in the crowd, not all of them as cheeky as the boy who asked for a kiss, were the chief beneficiaries of Diana's attention. As she knelt down to their level and chatted to them, it was evident from their thrilled expressions that she knew how to talk to even very young children in an entertaining and unpatronising way – a talent not given to all royals, or all adults for that matter.

So in a very few years, starting from scratch and with a shy temperament not, apparently, well equipped to handle the peculiar pressures of royal public life, Diana had turned herself from a hesitant amateur into a true professional. If Charles had been proud of her to start with, he had good

cause to be even more so now. Wherever the couple went – on tour to Italy, where they met the Pope, to America, Austria, back to Australia, to Japan, Hungary, Spain, Portugal, France, the Gulf States, Thailand, Hong Kong – the welcome they received was joyous and heartfelt. Millions turned out to catch a glimpse of the glamorous Diana and her prince. Adulation, of course, is heady stuff and there was a certain amount of hysteria present on some of Charles and Diana's overseas visits. This, though, was an inevitable result of extraordinary fame which in its turn was the natural corollary of international media coverage made possible by the high-tech revolution of the 1980s. Never before had royal faces been so familiar to people worldwide, and not royal faces carefully

Diana and children always make a good team. She knows how to talk to them in a natural way, so that the grand lady visitor, as she seems from a child's point of view, becomes an interesting friend. Here, Diana talks to some Australian youngsters in their playground. (ABOVE)

Charles walks with a Maori chief at his side towards the Treaty Grounds and Whore Runanga at Wallangi, New Zealand. The darts Charles carries were placed at his feet by a Maori warrior. He has picked them up to show he has acknowledged the challenge. (RIGHT)

Diana sits in a war canoe flanked by Maori warriors at Waitangi during the tour of New Zealand in 1983. The Maoris, the original natives of New Zealand, wear their traditional ceremonial dress and ornaments. They are about to row the royal couple to a Maori gathering. (OVERLEAF)

posed or viewed from a decorous distance, either. Camera technology enabled views of the royals so close up that the texture of their skin could be seen and the words on their lips read. It brought a new, intrusive dimension to royal-watching and both fed and escalated an insatiable interest. Even the most extensive tours undertaken by members of the Royal Family in pre-Diana days were sedate by comparison.

Unfortunately, as Diana-mania gained in impetus, it also threatened to run out of control and nurture far too much rumour and gossip. Most of it was as insubstantial as the air out of which it was, presumably, plucked, but it was persistent. The more pleasant tales speculated on Diana's next pregnancy and she only had to look tired or become dizzy from excessive heat, as happened in Vancouver, for rumours of another baby to start up again. The slightest coincidence fed the speculation. For instance, when Diana journeyed from Scotland to London on the same day that her gynaecologist returned to his Harley Street consulting rooms from holiday, the press put two and two together and got their arithmetic hopelessly wrong. Diana was not going to Harley Street about a third pregnancy, but to her dress designers for a fitting.

Gossip like this was, of course, easy to ignore and Diana had only to let enough time pass to prove rumour wrong. It was much more difficult, though, with the more insidious tales because, like the rest of the Royal Family, Charles and Diana cannot answer back to refute rumours or put straight a record distorted by wagging

tongues. Originally intended as a defence for the royals to enable them to rise above controversy and keep their dignity, this tradition also enabled gossip and innuendo to run free. Some of it was just plain perverse. Diana's figure – reed-slim, svelte and elegant – was widely admired, yet talk surfaced that she was suffering from anorexia nervosa, a serious condition which can, at its extreme, result in

Diana makes an enchanting picture in a pretty pink evening gown and simple jewellery, just a pearl necklace and earrings, when she went to see the New Zealand Ballet gala of *Coppélia* in April 1983.

Charles addresses a gathering of children at Eden Park in Auckland, New Zealand, in 1983. Around his neck he wears a Maori-style medallion. (RIGHT)

death. Diana's wardrobe, obviously expensive, extensive and exclusive, had long been a focus of great attention. Yet the anorexia allegations were soon followed by charges that Diana was splurging Charles's money on monster spending sprees at clothes and other shops in London's Knightsbridge, aided and abetted by her mother.

The gossip, founded on half-truths, inferences, incidents and comments taken out of context and often sheer invention, turned really nasty when doubts were cast on the survival of Charles and Diana's marriage. This was where the press, for whatever

Diana has a word with members of the Queen Victoria Maori Girls' School Cultural Group while visiting Eden Park, Auckland, on the New Zealand tour of 1983. (RIGHT)

A family reunion in New Zealand. While Charles and Diana were on tour, Prince Edward was working as a college tutor. Charles and his youngest brother were reunited and posed with Diana for a picture likely to go into the royal family album. (BELOW)

Diana looking serious as befits the occasion when she attends an Anzac Day service in New Zealand, held to commemorate the thousands of Australians and New Zealanders who died fighting in the two world wars and other conflicts. The flower pinned on Diana's dress is a poppy, a symbol of war commemorations ever since the First World War ended in 1918.

perverse reason, turned against the couple with a vengeance. Even the Queen and Prince Philip, in their time, had been obliged to endure such tittle-tattle and more recently the marriage of Prince and Princess Michael of Kent was rumoured to be in trouble with reports that the princess had, apparently, fallen for another man. Diana, for so long the golden girl who spread charm and friendliness all around, now had to put up with the same insidious treatment. She was an unsatisfactory wife and a shrew who did not shrink from quarrelling with Charles in public, making him look pathetic and hen-pecked. She was, it seemed, determined to take charge of the Wales household and get rid of Charles's friends and employees such as Stephen Barry, Charles's long-time

valet, and two personal detectives who had been with the prince for years. Certainly there were departures and changes among the Wales staff and it was unlikely that Diana would prove a passive decoration as wife, with no ideas and no contribution of her own to make to the household arrangements. This, though, was not what the gossip was saying. It was painting her as a petulant shrew who had made enemies all round. She had driven some forty individuals from royal service, alien-ated Princess Anne and Princess Margaret and practically emasculated Charles.

Much of the talk could have been exposed as the piffle it really was had anyone bothered to consult Charles and Diana's diaries to see the separate arrangements made for them, in the

Charles and Diana meet the Maoris during their tour of New Zealand in 1983. This meeting is friendly, but on other tours the Maoris have not hesitated to use the presence of the royals to publicise their griev-ances over their land rights in New Zealand.

There is no doubt how the people of St John's, Newfoundland in Canada, felt about the arrival of Charles and Diana in 1983. The royal couple are shown leaving the City Hall at St John's with band playing and two lines of uniformed guards flanking their path. (RIGHT)

WELCOME

natural course of their work, or the incidence of term times when Diana had to leave Charles to see their children safely back to school. The gossip, of course, included 'other men' for Diana who were in reality long-standing friends with whom she spent an evening or two out, always in the company of others. Even this, however, was not the peak of invention. The most outrageous tale of all whispered that Diana was nagging Charles to persuade his mother to abdicate so that she, Diana, could be queen. In these circumstances, it was difficult to know which of them had to put up with the greater insults. Charles was depicted as a hapless husband, unable to stop his wife reconstructing his life along her own preferred lines. Diana, apparently, led a double life, charming, modest and friendly in public, but power-hungry, a termagant and a troublemaker at home. The couple, it was suggested, had nothing at all in common except for their children, and Charles, it seems, was willing to stay away even from them in order to avoid Diana. That at least was an interpretation put upon the time they spent apart during 1987, when they were in separate locations on their sixth wedding anniversary.

This unsavoury chatter is familiar to many famous people who have found themselves raised up as idols one moment, only to be torn down the next. Fortunately, being insubstantial in the first place, rumour soon runs out of steam. Charles and Diana did the best possible thing while waiting for it to lapse. They said nothing, indicated less and changed no plans where

change might give the talk dignity. As a result, they emerged intact, even though they had had to endure two very difficult years between 1985 and 1987.

This unpleasant period in their lives was all the more distressing because the tide of innuendo had all but concealed the devotion which both Charles and Diana continued to lavish on their public service and their various patronages. They might be two contrasting personalities – Charles serious-minded, reflective,

Charles enjoys a quiet moment on his own before replying to an address of welcome from the Prime Minister of Alberta, Canada, Peter Longheed, in 1983. Diana looks on, standing next to Mrs Longheed.

While touring Canada in 1983, Charles and Diana were shown a range of local goods at the Edmonton Convention Centre which was set up for Universiade, 1983. (ABOVE)

While in Canada in 1983, Charles and Diana dressed up in costumes of 1878 to visit Fort Edmonton. Here they are flanked by Mounties, after coming out of a typical wooden building of the old fort, Charles in frock coat and pin-stripes, Diana in a long demure ruched gown and tip-tilted hat. (LEFT)

even austere and much given to philosophical musings, Diana more lighthearted and fun-loving – but there is no doubt that a vast area of concern exists which both of them share: to work for the welfare of ordinary people, especially the underprivileged, the disabled and the sick.

As Prince Charles himself once put

it, 'There is so much to be done in this world, so much famine exists, so much conflict, bigotry and prejudice, and there are so many people crying out for help, for their own simple dreams to come true'.

The royals, with their fame, their influence, their contacts and the privileges they enjoy, have a fine instrument for getting things done and are in a unique position to give that help. Good works may not make the same eye-catching headlines as are earned by the more glamorous public appearances of members of the Royal Family, but they are the solid base on which royal reputations are built. The Queen Mother once described their work and obligations as the rent that had to be paid for the space the royals occupied in life, and

both Charles and Diana have taken this dictum very much to heart.

There are, all the same, certain limits. By tradition, the British Royal Family may not become involved in politics at home or abroad, or in controversial issues. Certainly they may not express opinions about such matters in public, but the dividing line is thin and both Prince Philip and Prince Charles have on occasion been slapped on the wrist for comments that touched on tricky issues. Philip, however, advised his eldest son that 'Occasionally, you've got to stick your neck out'.

Diana's blue and white striped dress has a distinctly nautical air, complete with jaunty hat, as she arrives at Parliament Hill, Ottawa, while on tour with Charles in Canada in June 1983. (OVERLEAF)

Tree planting at Prince George in Canada. Charles and Diana seem to be getting two Canadian government ministers to do most of the work as they prepare to plant a tree to commemorate their visit in 1986.

Charles, fortunately, has long been in a good position to know where and how to stick out his neck. As heir to the throne, he has no specific role to play in the royal or even the national scheme of things, except to stand by as a king in waiting. This may seem a disadvantage, putting Charles at a loose end and without purpose in life, at least until he succeeds to the throne.

At the same time, though, it is advantageous because it leaves him free to choose his own sphere of action and he is well equipped to make the choice because of the regular input of knowledge he receives. Next to the Queen, Charles is the best-informed person in the country. Like his mother, he receives information in depth, much of it confidential, through his daily 'boxes'.

These contain Home Office reports; records of discussions and decisions in Cabinet, parliamentary and foreign affairs; coverage of industrial, social and economic matters throughout the country, and much else that gives Charles insight into the workings of British society. With all this at his disposal, together with his own experience, observations and a network of

Diana hangs on to her hat as she and her husband prepare to leave Canada for England on 1st July 1983. It was her twenty-second birthday and on the flight home there was a champagne party with two cakes. One was from the crew; the other was from Charles and in icing it said: 'I love you, darling'. (TOP)

Charles and Diana exchange a private word while watching a concert at Lobster Shanty North in Montague, Canada. In this picture, Diana is wearing her engagement ring, a sapphire surrounded by diamonds. (ABOVE)

specialist contacts which he has built up over the years, Charles is in the best position to pick out those areas that most need his attention.

Charles was quick to pinpoint conservation, environmental pollution and the problems of inner city living as important spheres for his efforts. His involvement began as long ago as 1968 when, at twenty, he was still a university undergraduate. The following year, 1969, was to be European Conservation Year and Charles agreed to chair the Welsh steering committee that was to mastermind the contribution of his principality. At the end of the year, Charles struck out on his own and formed the Prince of Wales Committee to raise funds for and oversee conservation projects in Wales. Charles's awareness of other people's feelings showed in his insistence that any scheme undertaken by the committee must first have the support of

As Diana looks on, Charles signs the guest book on their arrival at Central Park in Burnaby, Canada, in May 1986. (ABOVE)

Charles and Diana were joined by Mr Brian Mulroney PC MP and Mrs Mulroney when they attended a Government of Canada and Government of British Columbia dinner in 1986. (BELOW)

Charles and Diana fly in to Washington DC during their visit to the United States in 1985. The aircraft which brought them was a Royal Australian Air Force Boeing 707. The royal couple had been on their second visit to Australia, although this time Prince William was not with them as he had been on their first tour two years before. (RIGHT)

local residents. Once obtained, projects large and small went ahead. They ranged from a scheme by Pontypridd schoolchildren to lay a path of duckboards across marshes, to an international work camp at Aberfan. The work of Charles's committee goes on along the same lines over twenty years later and today, thanks to the prince and his initiatives, it has become a major factor in conservation in Wales.

Today, of course, conservation and similar concerns are much-publicised and much-discussed matters of on-going public interest, but it was not always like that. Prince Philip was termed an 'eco-nut' when he first embraced environmental problems and Charles has had to take some of the same flak. However, the royals' position is so secure in itself that they can afford to be prophets in the wilderness for however long it takes for public opinion to catch up with them.

This shows how members of the Royal Family can provide a lead and set standards of concern, yet also find thorns laid in the path of their efforts.

This royal occupational hazard arose again when Charles turned his attention to inner city problems, where youngsters were growing up in squalid, deprived environments that led them almost inevitably into lives of crime. Charles was deeply shocked when he first learned of this situation in 1972 and at once began planning how he could help. What he had discovered was a gap left by the Duke of Edinburgh's Award Scheme, founded in 1957, which rewarded youthful enterprise and innovation. However, the alienated young of the city ghettos lacked the motivation and self-regard which attracted others to the scheme. Charles realised early on that somehow they had to be infused with the sense of purpose and sense of community which was so signally absent from their lives: only then would they be able to help themselves.

While in Washington, Prince Charles addressed staff and guests at the National Gallery of Art where the royal couple viewed a special exhibition, 'The Treasure Houses of Britain'. (LEFT)

The United States freed itself from the rule of King George III and Britain during the American War of Independence two centuries ago. Seven generations later, Americans were only too delighted to welcome Prince Charles, King George's direct descendant, when he visited with his beautiful young wife in 1985. Royalty, in fact, has an enormous following of fans in the United States. Here, in a picture taken at the north portico of the White House, US President Ronald Reagan and his wife Nancy pose between Charles and Diana before going in to dinner. (RIGHT)

Charles and Diana arrive by air at the start of their Italian tour in 1985. Air travel has revolutionised the business of royal tours, enabling royals to visit several countries in one area within a short time. Royal tours of the past, undertaken by ship and train, took much longer and were more like expeditions. (ABOVE)

Rendezvous with the ancient past. During their tour of Italy, Charles and Diana took their places on a row of seats at the Greek-style theatre near Dorsenna del Canale. Here, hundreds of years ago, people watched Greek dramas performed by actors who wore huge masks to indicate the part – tragic or comic – which they were playing. The masks also acted like megaphones. It was a reflective moment for Charles, who has a great interest in archaeology. (RIGHT)

Even on a busy tour, there can be time for a private moment. Charles and Diana have a quiet word together during a break in their public engagements in Italy. (INSET)

Diana wore a cute head-topping nautical hat when she arrived at La Spezia, Italy, in April 1985, to be welcomed on the quayside. (LEFT)

On the way to meet Pope John Paul II at the Vatican. Fashion was left behind for the occasion as Diana wears the quiet black outfit with long lace veil traditional for women when received by the pontiff. Catholics were delighted with Diana's diplomatic gesture, although this is nothing unusual for her. When touring the Gulf States in 1989, she wore the trousers and long shift traditional for women in that area, as a diplomatic compliment to her Arab hosts. (LEFT)

Charles shows Diana the sights while on their tour of Italy. Even Diana is outdone by the traditional uniform with brilliant stripes worn by the guard standing, halberd in hand, outside the main building of the Vatican. (ABOVE)

The royal yacht *Britannia* sails majestically by the gondola-posts in Venice, the city where the streets are waterways. Italy, with its long coastline, made Charles and Diana's visit a combination of tour and cruise.

The Church, the police, the probation and social services and welfare organisations who were already battling with inner city deprivation and decay looked on Prince Charles's interest as a godsend. All the same, Charles was obliged to proceed quietly because, at first, many people considered the whole area too controversial. Some even voiced the opinion that

While in Italy, Charles and Diana visited Syracuse Harbour. Diana wore one of her most romantic hats for the occasion, a pink creation with a furled wavy brim.

Where royals go, security men are never far behind. Security for Charles and Diana, as for all the royals, has had to be stepped up in recent years and nothing is neglected in the quest to ensure their safety. Here, a skin-diver searches the waters during the royal tour of Italy, looking for obstructions and any other dangerous objects.

A ride by gondola was a must for Charles and Diana while they were in Venice. The gondoliers put on their best finery in honour of the royal couple as they steered them expertly along the famous Venetian canals. (LEFT)

getting involved with juvenile delinquents, many of whom already had a long list of convictions and a history of violence, was an unsavoury side of British life from which the prince ought to distance himself.

Charles, of course, thought otherwise, and it was an earnest reflection of his sincerity that the first schemes were financed from his own pay, then £5,000 a year as an officer in the Royal Navy. Groups of advisers were set up initially in Wales and Cornwall, where Charles had direct connections as prince and duke. The early requests the advisers received were pitifully modest and revealed even further the extent of the deprivation. One group of juveniles, who had already been in trouble with the police, wanted to go camping, but lacked almost everything they needed – tents, cooking utensils, bedding, even the money for their rail fares. A grant from Charles's navy pay bought their rail tickets, and Charles's influence produced a tent, utensils and other necessaries, all lent by the army. Later, Charles was gratified to learn that the holiday had been the making of the group. Having found someone who cared, which Charles certainly did, and backed up care with practical help, the group responded positively, relinquished their former truant ways and began attending school regularly.

Charles was too canny to expect miraculous conversions in all cases, but the need for a scheme like his quickly became evident as requests began to pour in. By 1976 committees

had been set up in seven more regions, by 1979 there were eight more and by 1987 another forty-six. In 1987 the undertaking, the Prince's Trust, became a registered charity aimed at helping young people between the ages of fourteen and twenty-five. The idea was to provide them with welfare and help in their personal development or their schemes to help others. To qualify, the young people had to be 'socially, economically or environmentally disadvantaged or physically handicapped'.

Today, the work of the Prince's

Diana's evening dress looks like starbursts in a night sky, an eye-catcher she wore on a visit to the Palazzo Pitti in Florence.

Trust networks virtually the whole country. Far from grabbing something for nothing, another criticism levelled early on at the prince's project, most requests have been quite small, such as money for a bicycle to do a newspaper round, to buy a pair of skates or go on an adventure holiday. No one has yet needed more than £300, the sum given by the Trust to two young Rastafarians

Royal tours are not all enjoyment and celebration. Diana looked solemn and thoughtful on a visit to Anzio during the tour of Italy in 1985, and with good reason. Anzio, where Allied forces landed to meet ferocious German resistance in 1944 during the Second World War, saw many weeks of hard-fought battle and thousands of casualties on both sides. (LEFT)

As can be seen here in a picture taken in Milan, the British Union Jack was much in evidence during Charles and Diana's tour of Italy. Diana returned the compliment by wearing an outfit in the Italian flag colours of green, white and red shortly after her arrival in the country. (ABOVE, LEFT)

Charles and Diana meet Pope John Paul II at the Vatican. There was some concern that Charles, a future king and head of the Church of England, might attend a Catholic mass, but the Queen stepped in and refused to allow it. However, it was all smiles when the royal couple met the Pope and the encounter went some way towards the cause of ecumenism, closer relations between the Protestant and Catholic Churches. (ABOVE)

The royal yacht *Britannia* dressed overall in flags and bunting, moored at the quayside at Bari during Charles and Diana's tour of Italy. From Bari, the prince and princess sailed on to Venice. (LEFT)

who wanted to set up a photographic dark room.

In his own work for the Trust, Charles has not hesitated to venture personally into the roughest and most dangerous inner city areas or tread in places affected by the rabid violence of racial disturbances. In 1981, he toured Toxteth after the appalling riots that took place there, as well as Handsworth in Birmingham, scarred by similar disturbances the same year. There were fears that he was entering a lion's den, but he was, in the event, greeted with well-deserved appreciation and friendliness. It was heartwarming evidence of Charles's own belief that 'there is no power, but there

Pearl chokers, once a fashion promoted by a former Princess of Wales, later Queen Alexandra, came back into favour when Diana started wearing them again. In this picture, Diana's choker sets off the quiet outfit she wore in Italy in 1985. (ABOVE)

can be influence and influence is in direct ratio to the respect people have for you'.

Ultimately, by 1987, Charles had earned the well-deserved if unofficial title of Prince of the Inner Cities, not only for the work of his Trust but for further welfare schemes such as his Youth Business Initiative, Business in the Community, the Inner Cities Trust and, among others, his efforts to find homes for youngsters living rough on the streets. Charles was outraged when he saw them sleeping in cardboard boxes by the River Thames under Waterloo Bridge. He at once asked the Prince's Trust to search out premises in the Kennington area of London

Children usually get the task of presenting flowers to the Princess of Wales when she comes to visit. This little Austrian girl, pictured during Charles and Diana's visit to her country in 1986, is doing quite well. However, her friend seems to have something else of interest and Diana wants to know what it is, too. Stranger things have happened. At one presentation, the little girl handing over the bouquet seemed to think Diana ought to give it back and something of a battle ensued. (OVERLEAF, LEFT)

Diana arrives at the *Konzerthaus* during the royal visit to Austria in 1986 to attend a concert by the Philharmonia Orchestra, one of the finest orchestras in the world. (OVERLEAF, RIGHT)

where at least they could have a proper roof over their heads, and later a scheme got under way to convert houses which belonged to the Duchy of Cornwall into forty small units.

The ever-burgeoning work of the Trust had, of course, long ago outpaced Charles's naval income which in any case had ceased when he left the navy to help establish the Queen's Silver Jubilee Trust. Money was now required on a vast scale and fund raising was the obvious answer. This was where Diana's attachment to pop music and rock stars came in very useful. She was familiar with the big chart successes of the pop world and the groups who scored them. The stars themselves were enthusiastic to give their help, and the first concert in aid of the Prince's Trust was given by Status Quo in 1982. Within five years, fifteen fund-raising concerts had taken place, one of which, held in the summer of 1986, raised nearly £1.2 million in ticket sales, television fees, record sales and video rights. Others held the same year produced nearly £1m more, and though less advertised than in the early days, this form of fund raising continues today.

It was, of course, almost unprecedented for the stars of the royal and the pop music firmaments to unite in this fashion. Traditional eyebrows were

Diana in one of her more demure fashions. She wore this shining blue gown, with high puff sleeves and pointed waist and neckline, to a dinner at the British Embassy in Tokyo during the royal tour of Japan in 1986. (LEFT)

In Japan, Charles and Diana are introduced to actors who are fully made-up and costumed for a performance of kabuki theatre. Kabuki is a traditional form of theatre in Japan. (RIGHT)

Diana strolls through the luxuriant foliage of the Shugakuin gardens in Kyoto, during the tour of Japan in 1986. One of Charles's favourite re- laxations is painting and sketching and Japan, which has many beauties like this garden, gave him unprecedented opportunities. (ABOVE)

Charles and Diana take part in the famous Japanese tea ceremony while at a garden party at Nijo Castle, Kyoto, in 1986. The ceremony, which is conducted with much formal ritual, is a way of honouring and welcoming distinguished guests. (LEFT)

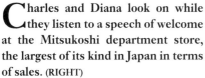

Charles and Diana look on while they listen to a speech of welcome at the Mitsukoshi department store, the largest of its kind in Japan in terms of sales. (RIGHT)

raised, despite the good cause, at this unusual juxtaposition and the royals' 'unseemly' exposure to showbiz razzmatazz. There was shock, too, when Bob Geldof, a pioneer of famine relief in Africa, turned up to see Charles at home in his usual state of scruffy disarray: three-day beard, uncombed locks, old jeans and crumpled T-shirt. Prince William, apparently, came into his father's study and demanded to know why this 'dirty man' was there. The same question was asked for far more snobbish reasons by a variety of critics.

Charles was no pop music fan. He preferred opera and once complained to friends that Diana had hijacked him to 'some sort of rock jamboree'. The comment was good-natured, though, and he genuinely admired Geldof's enterprise in tackling head-on the appalling suffering caused by war and poverty.

Even so, the rock world connection had its problems and for more serious reasons. Concern was voiced that

There's something interesting down there. Charles and Diana pause during their tour of the Shuga-kuin gardens in Kyoto. Japanese gardens are arranged to grow as if they were paintings, and their tour showed the prince and princess a piece of living art as well as beautiful horti-culture. Well, what was it? Diana seems to be looking to Charles for an explanation as two Japanese priests stand by.

Although the Japanese have a royal family of their own, they tend to be rather remote compared to Britain's royals. The Emperor of Japan officially renounced his divinity after the Second World War in 1945, but he is still regarded as a god by many Japanese. British royals are much more obviously human and approach-able. When Charles and Diana visited Japan, people flocked to see and greet them. In this picture, Charles is seen visiting Tofukugi monastery, part of the temple of Zen Buddhism built in 1235 at Kyoto, together with the chief priest Yenzan Yasuga and a crowd of eager companions. (RIGHT)

A bridge over a large artificial pond is a must in the traditional Japanese garden. Charles and Diana view their surroundings at the Shugakuin gardens, which date from 1659, with their guide.

Charles meets a sumo wrestler during his tour of Japan with Diana. Not surprisingly, there is something a bit tentative about Charles's smile as he views the tall and massively built wrestler, an exponent of a sport practised in Japan for many centuries and still very popular today. (BELOW)

Fashions old and new. Charles and Diana, who is wearing a striking two-colour outfit, meet a little Japanese girl dressed in a brightly coloured kimono. The kimono and its accompanying sash, or obi, was for centuries the traditional dress worn in Japan. (OVERLEAF)

Charles and Diana were consorting with pop stars, such as Boy George, who were known drug users. The critics need not have been concerned. Socialising with the likes of Boy George did not prevent Diana speaking out several times, and strongly, over the fearsome problems of drug-taking among the young.

Ruffled establishment feathers were, however, soothed by other causes embraced by Diana which proved to be much more in line with tradition. As is appropriate, Diana has concentrated on the feminine side of royal patronage and had barely settled in as Princess of Wales before scores of requests reached her to become president of this or patron of that. It was impossible for her to accept them all, but within four or five years, she had built up a portfolio of eighteen patronages, which then seemed a realistic number for a princess intent on not only giving her name to but her active participation in the organisations within her sphere. Nevertheless, by 1990, the number of Diana's patronages had risen to over thirty.

Children, her enduring interest, naturally figure prominently in Diana's work. The best-known children's charity with a Diana connection is Dr Barnardo's Homes, of which she is president. In this context, Diana was able to show how a charity 'do' can

Diana gets to feel what it is like to wear the traditional Japanese kimono, even though she is nearly a foot taller than the average Japanese woman. This kimono was specially made for her by the Kimono Makers Association of Kyoto.

have glamour when, in March 1985, a spectacular fashion show was held in London's Grosvenor House Hotel featuring dresses designed by Bruce Oldfield, a former Barnardo boy. On that occasion Diana, wearing a magnificent silver dress designed for her by Oldfield, was a walking advertisement for him. The money the show raised went, of course, to the orphanage.

Diana performs similar functions for the Pre-School Playgroups Association, the National Deaf, Blind and Rubella Association, and also Help the Aged, of which she is patron. The complete list of organisations that can claim Diana's sanction and time is very long – as early as 1985, it occupied ten pages or more on the Buckingham Palace records of royal patronages – and it penetrates not only into the area of child care, but also of health. Diana is, to give a few examples, either patron or president of the Malcolm Sargent Cancer Fund for Children, the British Lung Foundation, Birthright, the Royal Anthropological Institute, the National Meningitis Trust, Royal Marsden Hospital in London and Relate, which deals with family problems.

With this level of involvement, Diana's diary necessarily fills up quickly. During three weeks in September and October 1990 alone, Diana undertook nine engagements connected with her patronages and five others of a general nature, and September was a short month for her. Because of her tour of Pakistan which, as it happened, was cancelled due to political unrest, Diana's timetable was cut down from its usual level of activity.

Although Diana, like Charles and the rest of the Royal Family, has schedules planned at least six months in advance or, in the case of overseas

tours, a year ahead or more, they still find time for the unplanned gesture. One such was Diana's impromptu visit in September 1990 to the self-help organisation set up to aid hostages caught in the crisis which followed Iraq's invasion of Kuwait the previous month. The sudden disaster, such as the storm damage that hit Wales and elsewhere in the wake of the hurricane of 1987, or the Hillsborough football stadium disaster of 1989, also requires the royals to react fast. Both Charles and Diana were on the scene of both tragedies within days to comfort the bereaved and injured and offer sympathy and support. Also, on more than one occasion, Diana has not been afraid to risk controversy by spontaneous decisions of her own. In 1989, for example, she broke taboos by visiting a children's AIDS ward while on a visit to New York. Later the same year, while on tour in the Far East, she asked to be taken to a leper hospital where she held hands with the unfortunates who suffered from a disease which, since biblical times, has condemned them as 'unclean' and untouchable. Gestures like this do more to dispel fear and ignorance than years of propaganda and appeals to humanity.

Normally, though, the appearance of Charles, Diana or both at a public engagement marks the end of long preparation and planning. Timetables must be prearranged – vital for the

Charles and Diana arrive at Bangkok airport at the start of their tour of Thailand in 1988. The big umbrellas provided much-needed shade, for the Thai climate can be very hot and humid, and dressing to keep cool is difficult on formal occasions like this. Diana, unfortunately, suffers in high temperatures, though etiquette demands that royals must not be seen to wilt in the heat. (OVERLEAF)

Diana watches as Charles signs the guest book at the Emerald Buddha Temple in Bangkok, capital of Thailand, during their visit in February 1988. (PREVIOUS SPREAD, LEFT)

Charles and Diana are dwarfed by the ornate splendours of the Emerald Buddha Temple, which they visited during their first and so far only tour of Thailand in 1988. (PREVIOUS SPREAD, RIGHT)

multi-visit days out when there are more than one or two places to be covered – security has to be minutely checked out, travel arrangements made. Charles and Diana need to be briefed on the places they will see, the people they will meet, the ceremonies they may have to perform or the extent and location of the walkabout. The almost clinical minute-by-minute precision required is considerable and nothing is left to chance. Like all royal ladies, Diana brings an invaluable aid with her whenever she appears in public: her lady-in-waiting, whose capacious handbag contains a sewing

kit for emergency repairs, some tissues and, among sundry other items, a copy of Diana's speech if she has to make one.

Tours abroad are a similar undertaking but greatly magnified, a mammoth moving royal show where the smallest detail must be arranged well in advance. Some of Charles's staff go out to discuss security and make sure the local press know how to approach the prince and princess, and warn them off asking political or personal questions. They liaise with various hosts, make arrangements for the functions the royal couple will attend,

At a factory in the north of Thailand, Diana contemplates the beautifully decorated umbrellas which are a feature of the markets in Chiang Mai. (LEFT)

Charles and Diana had lots to talk about after visiting the complex of temples in Bangkok's Grand Palace. They did not wait to make a start, as this picture shows. Thailand is full of beautiful, exotic green- and red-roofed temples and there, even the much-travelled royals found plenty to marvel at. (OVERLEAF)

Prince Charles regularly appears in uniform in public, and has a large wardrobe of uniforms to wear on various occasions. This is not only because of the time he himself spent in the armed services, but because, like other members of the Royal Family, he is honorary head of several regiments and other corps. Charles is seen here arriving at Port Moresby, Papua, in 1984.

check guest lists and organise ceremonies. At home, preparations for the tour are no less complex. Tons of baggage must be organised, including suitable wardrobes for the royal couple, with suits, uniforms, dresses and all accessories for every occasion, gifts and scores of signed photographs that need to be handed out and also sombre reminders of mortality: mourning clothes in case of a royal death while Charles and Diana are away, and for Charles, the documents he might have to sign if, like his mother in 1952, he unexpectedly becomes sovereign while far from home.

The essence of this enterprise is that whether Charles and Diana are touring separately or together, at home or abroad, the whole scheme has to fit into the royal calendar which encompasses the schedules followed by the rest of the Royal Family. One of the reasons Diana in 1981, and in 1986 Miss Sarah Ferguson, were unable to

The Prince of Wales has to join in many ceremonies and celebrations important to different cultures overseas and he has many unusual presents at home to prove it. Here he is in 1984 in Papua New Guinea, a Pacific territory which is part of the British Commonwealth, wearing the crossed garlands and crown of a supreme chief on the island of Manus. Charles was given this new honour while he was in Papua New Guinea to open a new Parliament building. (LEFT)

Charles, a garland of welcome made from exotic flowers around his neck, views displays at the Kangere Community Centre in Papua in August 1984. (RIGHT)

Charles and Diana made a brief stop-over at the romantic Pacific island of Hawaii on their way from Australia to the United States in 1985. They were duly decorated with the garlands which say 'welcome to the island'. (ABOVE)

Ladies-in-waiting such as Anne Beckwith-Smith, seen here with Diana in Canada, often become close friends of the royals they serve. Miss Beckwith-Smith was Diana's first full-time lady-in-waiting and accompanied her on her earliest tours abroad, as well as at home. (LEFT)

Diana's first official solo engagement abroad was a weekend in Norway in 1984, where she attended a performance of *Carmen* given by the London City Ballet, of which she is patron. Diana has always loved ballet and as a child she wanted to be a ballet dancer. She grew to be far too tall, however. (RIGHT)

exercise the bride's privilege of picking their own wedding day was that all royal diaries had to be consulted first to find a day when everyone who should be there, could be there.

Other events where Charles and Diana may join the rest of the Royal Family are fortunately more predictable. There are two main cycles: royal holidays – that is, Balmoral in the summer and Christmas at Sandringham or Windsor – and social or national events for which the royals usually turn out in force. There is the Chelsea Flower Show in May, Ascot Week in June, Cowes in July, the Trooping the Colour parade, the Sovereign's Official Birthday parade, the royal garden parties held at Buckingham Palace, several investitures, the Royal Opening of Parliament and, more sombrely, the ceremony at the Cenotaph in Whitehall in November where the royals pay their tributes to Britain's war dead. These staples of the royal year do not take account of variables, such as state visits by kings, queens, presidents and other distinguished personages from overseas, where the heir to the throne must play his part in the royal welcome.

However glittering and enjoyable all this may sometimes appear, royal engagements are not jaunts. They have a serious purpose, or rather several, which together form an important diplomatic service for the country. Quite apart from their own charitable and social concerns at home in Britain, Charles and Diana have to do their bit to cement overseas relations, boost trade, bolster the Commonwealth and generally act as ambassadors for Britain.

Diana has made a few experiments with her hair style over the years. Her blonde tresses have come in short, medium and long styles and here, at an evening engagement in Australia in 1988, she wore her hair up with a decorative star at the back, the sort of ornament more often connected with Diana's close friend, the Duchess of York.

During her early public appearances, Diana wore many small head-topping hats, like this crimson creation which suited her youth and also provided for the royal rule that hats should preferably not conceal the face. This picture was taken in 1983 when Diana attended a luncheon given by the Variety Club of Great Britain at the Guildhall in aid of Sunshine Coaches. (RIGHT)

Diana 'wowed' Americans when she and Charles toured the United States in November 1985. Here she is in Washington, the capital of the United States, in a striking one-shouldered evening gown. In royal terms, it was daring. No wonder the Americans were impressed.

This smart hat, designed to provide Diana with some shade from the hot Australian sun during her third tour in 1988, resembles the planet Saturn with its many rings, appropriate royal headgear for the space age.

Pretty picture, pretty princess. Diana dressed quietly with a minimum of jewellery for her first visit to the AIDS Actors 'Landmark' Centre in Lambeth, London, in July 1989. Diana has been foremost among British royals in rallying support for sufferers from this dreaded new disease, a courageous stand in an area of much prejudice and fear. (RIGHT)

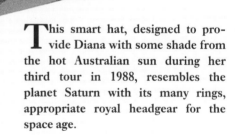

Men's evening wear was the inspiration behind this outfit which Diana wore in Italy in 1985. Secure in her role as queen of fashion, Diana likes to be innovative from time to time and in royal terms, she explored new ground here. Because of Diana and her clothes designers, most of them young and full of new ideas, royal fashion has become a popular talking point in the last ten years. (LEFT)

Diana favoured a demure country girl image when she wore this off-the-shoulder black and white dress to London's Barbican in September 1989. (BELOW)

Red all the way. In 1985, Diana brightened up a grey day in Florence during her tour of Italy with Charles when she wore matching stockings to complement her red outfit. (OVERLEAF)

However, despite their frequent appearances at state, charity or other functions, their speeches and actions in support of a variety of good causes and the genuine love they earn from ordinary people, Prince Charles has often been accused of having 'no proper job'. This presumably includes Diana, too. This is grossly unfair to a hard-working couple who have little time left for a private life of their own once royal duties are done. The task they perform, whether separately or together, may have no specific job description, but it has many labels, not the least of which say 'service', 'devotion' and 'dedication'. In that context their first ten years together, which are marked in 1991, certainly give ample cause for celebration.

A plain scoop neck shows off a beautiful matching necklace and earring set in this shimmering midnight-blue dress which Diana wore during her tour of Austria in 1986. (LEFT)

S heer glamour. Diana wore this scintillating red gown for a date at London's Waldorf Hotel in July 1989. (RIGHT)

D iana works hard to keep a slim figure which this red and blue outfit she wore in 1986 shows off admirably. Since her engagement in 1981, she has dieted down two dress sizes, helped by regular exercise, swimming, dancing and playing tennis. (OVERLEAF, LEFT)

A woman has to be as slim as bamboo for this. In Australia in 1985, Diana showed how it was done when she wore this brilliant-red evening gown with wide shoulders, which tapered down to her ankles in an inverted triangle. (OVERLEAF, RIGHT)

As Charles and Diana danced at the Melbourne Mayoress's Ball during their
1985 tour of Australia, the band was appropriately playing Stevie Wonder's
'Isn't She Lovely?'.